MANAGING HIGHER EDUCATION AS A BUSINESS

by
Robert L. Lenington

AMERICAN COUNCIL ON EDUCATION ★
ORYX PRESS ★
Series on Higher Education
1996

The rare Arabian Oryx is believed to have inspired the myth of the unicorn. This desert antelope became virtually extinct in the early 1960s. At that time several groups of international conservationists arranged to have 9 animals sent to the Phoenix Zoo to be the nucleus of a captive breeding herd. Today the Oryx population is over 1000, and over 500 have been returned to the Middle East.

© 1996 by American Council on Education and The Oryx Press
Published by The Oryx Press
4041 North Central at Indian School Road
Phoenix, Arizona 85012-3397

Published simultaneously in Canada
Printed and Bound in the United States of America

∞ The paper used in this publication meets the minimum requirements of American National Standard for Information Science—Permanence of Paper for Printed Library Materials, ANSI Z39.48, 1984.

Library of Congress Cataloging-in-Publication Data
Lenington, Robert L.
    Managing higher education as a business / by Robert L. Lenington.
        p. cm. — (American Council on Education/Oryx Press series on higher education)
    Includes bibliographical references and index.
    ISBN 1-57356-023-5 (alk. paper)
    1. Education, Higher—United States—Administration.
2. Education, Higher—United States—Business management.
I. Title. II. Series.
LB2341.L426 1996
378'.1'0973—dc20   96-7617
                                                                              CIP

CONTENTS

• • • • • • • • •

FOREWORD

• • • • • • • • •

F ew would argue that higher education is very much a part of the American dream. Parents, students, and members of the higher education community share certain common images: young people moving on to college after completing high school, seats reserved for those who survive a highly selective screening process, finding a way to somehow meet high tuition costs, and good jobs awaiting those who graduate. Unfortunately those familiar with higher education know that the reality is quite different.

Several factors have come together in the 1990s to create serious challenges for most colleges and universities. Widespread tuition discounting has destabilized higher education's single most important revenue source. The structure and amount of federal support to higher education, both in the form of student aid and research money, continue to change. Only a small number of institutions have sufficiently large endowments to provide meaningful support to current operations. The pool of 18-year-olds continues to shrink, and few see a return to "baby boom" enrollment levels even when the current trend reverses by the end of the decade. In addition to these issues, which are somewhat unique to higher education, colleges and universities are also faced with more universal issues like managing downsizing costs, maintaining their physical plants, and funding benefit costs.

Conventional approaches to dealing with these issues are, for the most part, ineffective or simply not available. Traditionally, institutions have simply raised their tuition to fund their costs, but many parents will argue that the aggregate charges have crossed the line of what they can pay. Financial aid provides some relief but often not enough to make a difference. Alternatively, institutions have increased enrollment, but this approach is often not practicable either. Many schools are already accepting most who apply and still not filling their classes. Competition and unfavorable demographics stand in the way of increasing enrollments.

It is difficult to predict with certainty what effects these issues will ultimately have on American higher education, but it is easy to speculate. The strongest and best managed institutions will likely find creative solutions to these issues and thrive. Indeed, many such institutions continue to be extremely selective in admitting students and still fill their seats. Weak and poorly managed institutions will probably disappear. Some will be absorbed by other schools, and some will simply close their doors, perhaps under the oversight of a bankruptcy court. The rest of the institutions will continue on in a fashion that few will find satisfactory.

There are no simple or magic solutions to these issues. It would be imprudent to assume, however, that a strong economy or the federal government will provide solutions. The issues are more fundamental than that. Many knowledgeable observers would agree that any solution will need to focus, to a significant degree, on the financial underpinnings of our colleges and universities. The economic reality is that the bills have to be paid. Academic excellence counts for little if an institution cannot fill its seats or fund its research activities. Conversely, sound financial management can create opportunities to attract outstanding faculty and students.

Managing Higher Education as a Business is intended to stimulate the thinking of its readers on ways to improve the financial management of institutions of higher education. The ideas presented are not based on empirical research. Rather, they reflect the candid observations of an individual who spent the last 16 years of his career at Bentley College, dealing directly with these issues as vice president for business and finance and as treasurer. Bentley is predominately oriented toward accounting and business education and enjoys a solid reputation for sound fiscal management—a repute earned in no small measure because of the contributions of the author. Bob Lenington's 16 years in higher education followed a 24-year career in industry. Indeed, Bob's ideas reflect the application of business principles learned early in his career, then adapted with success to higher education at Bentley. Unfortunately, higher education in general is an arena where such ideas have often been viewed as alien and threatening. Many of his ideas can result in greater productivity at reduced cost, allowing for more realistic pricing of tuition and fees.

We hope that this book will be read with interest by many different audiences within the higher education community, but we expect that it will have particular appeal to board members. Board members, many of whom are business executives, often focus on the question of why sound financial management principles should not be applied in the not-for-profit arena. Bob's message is that such principles must be applied.

Mark A. Quinn
Partner, Ernst & Young

INTRODUCTION

• • • • • • • •

The Changing Environment of Higher Education

n the last decade of this century, higher education in the United States has arrived at a crossroads regarding its ability to provide affordable access to its citizens. When did higher education begin having financial difficulty? Naturally, there was no particular date; but if I had to select one, I would suggest that serious difficulties started one bright sunny morning late in 1979. The country was then in the early stages of an extended period of double-digit inflation. Higher education, traditionally a cost-plus business, was caught up in the inflationary spiral like every other business in the country and responded to the problem with double-digit tuition increases.

Coincidental with this morning in late 1979, a 17-year demographic decline in the number of high school graduates started.[1] Although the country gained control of double-digit inflation and brought it down to a manageable level, higher education continued double-digit tuition increases for the balance of the decade.[2] For a while, Ma, Pa, and the kids found ways to handle the tuition increases once inflation came under control. In addition, more mothers were entering the workforce, increasing family income, and the 1980s witnessed the longest period of economic expansion since World War II.

A day of reckoning arrived in the first months of the 1990s. Revenue growth from tuition had slowed due to the declining pool of traditional 18-year-olds. The country was slipping into a major recession, the dual-income family trend had peaked, and 10 years of double-digit tuition increases were

---

[1]Thomas W. Langfitt, "The Costs of Higher Education: Lessons to Learn from the Health Care Industry," *Change* (November/December 1990): 11.

[2]Daniel T. Layzell and Jan W. Lyddon, *Budgeting for Higher Education at the State Level: Enigma, Paradox, and Ritual*, ASHE-ERIC Higher Education Report no. 4 (Washington, DC: The George Washington University, School of Education and Development, 1990), 59-60.

beginning to take their toll. Other factors complicated the situation. Because of its societal mission and designation as a not-for-profit business, higher education has always been governed more like a federal, state, or city government agency than a competitive business entity. Aggravating this condition was the fact that higher education has little offshore competition such as motivated American industries during the 1970s and 1980s to contain costs and provide competitive quality products.

The resources of higher education are exactly the same as the resources of any business entity: personnel, physical plant, and capital. When higher education learns how to manage its resources, it will be able to contain costs, improve productivity, and enhance nonstudent-related revenues. This book summarizes the factors that have created a runaway cost situation in higher education, presents chapters that explain the primary business/management features of the industry, and develops a long shopping list of changes that can be made in the conduct of business affairs to reinstate affordable access for all our citizens to higher education.

Higher education currently faces many individually troublesome problems that could collectively overwhelm many institutions. A selected list of these major problems is given below.

- The demographic decline of 18-year-olds, which started in 1979, entered its worst period of decline at the turn of the 1990s and will continue to be a problem late into the decade.
- Tuition costs have become prohibitive for an increasing number of families. Tuition costs rose faster the past 20 years than median income for the American family.[3] This condition will worsen during the next decade because median family income will not benefit from the dual-income buildup, which has matured.
- The federal government has reduced subsidies to higher education for financial aid relative to tuition cost. This problem was compounded when the government offered a greater reliance on debt relative to grants.[4]
- The federal government declared higher education's practice of sharing planned tuition, salary, and financial aid information to be a violation of antitrust law.[5]
- The federal government is constraining expenditures that research institutions include in their overhead pools for allocation to government-funded research projects. If certain costs are disallowed, al-

---

[3]Arthur M. Hauptman, *The Tuition Dilemma* (Washington, DC: The Brookings Institution, 1990), 2-5.

[4]Hauptman, *The Tuition Dilemma*, 7-10.

[5]Thomas J. Kerr, "College Tuition: Collusion or Compromise?," *School and College* (June 1990): 11-16.

though deemed appropriate by the institution, recovery of indirect expenditures in the research sector of higher education's business will be reduced. The resultant condition will impose a disproportionate amount of indirect costs onto the education sector of the business.[6]

- Many state governments, in response to their own fiscal and deficit problems, have reduced subsidies for state institutions of higher education and scholarship programs for private institutions. These reductions will raise tuition and fee rates at state institutions while reducing student capacity.[7] Private institutions will fail to replace lost scholarship funds, thereby reducing student access.

- City governments claim that facilities used by institutions to house students are unrelated to the institution's primary mission of education and should be subject to property taxes.

- Federal, state, and city governments are all becoming much more sensitive to unrelated business activities conducted on campuses. They feel that "for-profit" use of campus facilities for housing, feeding, or entertaining individuals or organizations unrelated to the mission of the institution should subject the institution to assessment of taxes, including federal, state, and city income, sales, property, and hotel taxes.[8] There is also a growing concern that these uses create unfair competition for local vendors, restaurants, and hotels because of the tax advantage enjoyed by institutions of higher education.

- Higher education has neglected its physical plant during the past 20 years. Deferred maintenance in the industry now amounts to approximately $75 billion, of which $25 billion is a critical deferment because it affects functionality and safety.[9] Although higher education has appealed to the federal government for support in addressing this accumulated deferred maintenance, Washington has not been receptive to mitigating this problem.

- Economic competition in a global economy will force salary containment in the United States to maintain relative productivity. This situation can only worsen the median family income to tuition ratio.

This book was developed to provide a financial/management overview of the industry known as higher education. This introduction on the changing

---

[6]Richard E. Anderson and Joel W. Meyerson, eds., *Financing Higher Education in a Global Economy* (New York: American Council on Education and Macmillan Publishing Company, 1990), 55-56.

[7]Connie Leslie, "The Public Ivy Is Withering," *Newsweek* (29 April 1991): 64-65.

[8]Anderson and Meyerson, *Financing Higher Education in a Global Economy*, 28.

[9]Kent John Chabotar and James P. Honan, "Coping with Retrenchment," *Change* (November/December 1990): 34.

environment of higher education and Part I, Background, on the factors responsible for unrealistic tuition increases will set the stage for the next four major parts of the book. Part II, Organization and Management, addresses the role of the board (Chapter 2) and organization options for the management of operations (Chapter 3). Part III, Strategic Overview, reviews strategic planning (Chapter 4), the relationship of strategic planning and the operating budget (Chapter 5), costing and pricing issues (Chapter 6), and marketing the institution (Chapter 7). Part IV, Revenue Sources, covers tuition, auxiliary enterprises, and other revenue opportunities (Chapter 8); fund raising and grants (Chapter 9); and investment management (Chapter 10). This entire section concentrates on the enhancement of revenues to compensate for a dwindling revenue flow from student-related activities. Part V, Major Expenditure Areas, reviews administration (Chapter 11), academics and faculty (Chapter 12), the physical plant (Chapter 13), and financial aid and other subsidies (Chapter 14). Chapter 14 highlights tuition price discounting, which expanded exponentially during the 1980s and will be a troublesome area during the balance of the 1990s. Part VI, Conclusions and Predictions, ends with a chapter of predictions on how the higher education environment may change.

Five major constituencies represent an institution of higher education: students, alumni, faculty, administrators, and management. This book concentrates on management, which includes the board members and officers of the institution. Four of the constituencies, including management, serve to address the primary constituency—the students. The societal mission of an institution of higher education is to educate the student. The student is the potential customer when recruited, a client for two, four, or more years while enrolled, and, upon graduation, the product of the industry of higher education.

After 350 years, higher education is entering a new era of serious competition. During the 1990s, many institutions will cease to exist, and others will merge to form stronger organizations. Higher education will learn that the customer is king.

An era of detailed strategic planning, competitive marketing, and professional management is in the process of developing in higher education. This book will provide a brief, relatively comprehensive overview of the intricacies of its business for senior management and board members.

PART

I

· · · · · · · · ·

Background

CHAPTER 1

· · · · · · · · ·

Factors Responsible for Unrealistic Tuition Increases

This chapter will lay the foundation for the book. I will review the changes in the higher education industry and American society that have contributed to higher education's runaway costs. No sector of the business will be spared an objective review. Some of opinions expressed may transgress what is euphemistically labeled "politically correct" on certain campuses in the 1990s. The balance of the book is devoted to suggesting ways to improve management of resources and realign the industry.

Contributing to the delay in addressing the rapid buildup of costs in higher education has been the advent during the past 20 years of the dual-income family. The availability of a second family income allowed for many inefficiencies in conducting the affairs of society's businesses. Where there was growing world competition, such as in American manufacturing industries, American firms were forced to address productivity and quality problems. With little offshore competition to higher education, however, costs continued to escalate unrealistically.

The management of higher education requires the same skills as management of industry. The basic resources are the same: personnel, capital, physical plant. Proper management and attention to these resources provide a stable foundation for any successful business, including higher education. Recognizing higher education as a business is of paramount importance if costs are to be brought under control and if affordable tuition is to be made available to everyone.

Higher education is in a difficult period because it is caught between a weak primary/secondary education system and a highly competitive and expanding global marketplace. Demographics complicate the problem; for the 17-year period 1979 through 1996, the number of 18-year-olds available to pursue higher education declined. However, the full impact of this decline was partially offset during the late 1970s and early 1980s by the women's movement, which resulted in more women seeking a college education than ever before.[1] In addition, more adult (nontraditional) students pursued education in the evenings, realizing that downsizing and reengineering efforts to improve productivity in industry would result in greater competition for professional positions. Recently, international students have been heavily recruited.

To date, higher education in the United States has succeeded in providing the finest education system in the world. However, higher education in other parts of the world may eventually meet or possibly surpass American standards, resulting in increasing numbers of American students opting for an education offshore where tuition costs may be appreciably less.

With the political structure and economies of most nations in the world changing rapidly, there is no reason to think that higher education in the United States will not be subjected to the same economic forces that affect other business sectors within the American economy. To maintain its standard of living, the U.S. will have to compete directly with foreign nations. The Asiatic nations, Japan in particular, are already competing head-on with our economy. Economic blocs, including those in Western and Eastern Europe, are developing, and soon China, with 25 percent of the world's population, will join the other economic powers of Asia. Most nations in the world appear to be evolving as democracies that will rely on free enterprise for the growth and development of their economies.

Competition is healthy and motivates people to be efficient. The challenge to education during the remainder of the 1990s will be to prepare for two potential sources of competition that have not existed before. First, as mentioned earlier, the education systems in other nations may develop to the point where significant numbers of our students opt to go abroad for their education. Second, the threat exists within our own boundaries that the for-profit business sector will take advantage of the evolving profit opportunity afforded by today's high tuition rates to set up proprietary institutions of higher education financed by stockholders or private money.

Having said this, let us proceed with a list of the major factors that have contributed to the extraordinary increases in tuition rates during the past 30 years.

---

[1]Pamela J. Perun, *The Undergraduate Woman: Issues in Educational Equity* (Lexington, MA: D.C. Heath & Company, 1982), 44-46.

ACADEMIC FACTORS

Instruction Costs

The business of higher education is instruction. Higher education is a labor-intensive business, and the faculty who provide the instruction and the personnel who support them represent the single largest expense for operating the institution. Not only are faculty and their instructional support the largest cost factor in an institution of higher education, but their costs have become the most troublesome factor contributing to unrealistic growth in tuition rates. What created cost problems was the parallel trends of reduced teaching loads and higher salaries in combination with smaller class sizes.[2] The result is a triple-faceted cost problem.

Faculty Salaries

Faculty members and their regional and national organizations have for many years collected salary data in detail by discipline and by faculty rank (e.g., instructor, assistant professor, associate professor, professor). Faculty were able to measure growth of their incomes relative to inflation. Armed with their statistics, faculty in the 1980s put pressure on all institutions to provide exceptional salary increases[3] to catch up on the salary base they perceived themselves to have lost during the years of inflation. In fact, few professions kept pace with inflation because individuals are not fully affected by the many inflationary factors included in the Consumer Price Index (CPI). Even the federal government has now recognized this issue.

Research

Research can be financed internally by the institution or externally by a third party, in which case the project is termed "sponsored research." Both forms of research create cost pressure on an institution. Internal research requires a diversion of internal funds, which forces tuition increases, to provide the funds. Sponsored research by third parties, such as the government, foundations, and industry, frequently does not compensate fully for all college costs incurred, particularly administrative overhead defined as indirect cost. In addition to government-, foundation-, and industry-sponsored research, there is a fourth area of research, usually financed by individuals whose contributed funds are endowed. These funds are established in perpetuity and also seldom provide for indirect cost recovery.

---

[2] Jeffrey L. Sheler et al., "A New Era on Campus," *U.S. News and World Report* (16 October 1989): 55.

[3] "Trends and Indicators," *The Chronicle of Higher Education* (25 March 1992): A16.

Student Affairs

Student Affairs, as a division separate from academics, was nonexistent 40 years ago. The heaviest expenditures for Student Affairs today are operation of the residence facilities, athletic/recreational programs, and personal/professional counseling activities.

Prior to World War II, resident supervision and counseling functions were handled by certain faculty as a part of their contractual obligation. The creation of departments within Student Affairs for resident activities and counseling added cost to the operation of an institution of higher education.

A second factor affecting student operations at many institutions is management assignment of auxiliary activities to the Student Affairs division. Auxiliary programs such as residential housing, food service, bookstore, summer camps, industry conferencing, service stores, and varsity programs are true business activities. Higher education has become progressively more dependent on the operating margin these businesses are capable of generating to subsidize instruction, the primary business of the institution. If the officer in charge of Student Affairs is not business trained, or teamed with the business officer, the institution may not realize margin opportunity.

Expansion of Library Capacity

Our quest for knowledge is insatiable. Today's technology provides the wherewithal to inundate the average individual with online databases. Higher education libraries provide data in the form of computer technology as well as increased book selection. Libraries have also responded to the "publish or perish" demands on faculty, which allegedly require large comprehensive on-site library facilities. All these needs are expensive and increase the cost of operating institutions of higher education.

ADMINISTRATIVE FACTORS

Additional Administrative Personnel

As our government representatives develop ever more opportunities for citizens to be employed by state and federal bureaucracies, Murphy's Many Laws provide expanding forms, statistics, and regulations to keep them busy.[4] Higher education responded over the past 20 years to these demands by dramatically adding administrative staff to fulfill the bureaucratic requirements. When the citizens of the country finally demand that taxes be con-

---

[4]William F. Massy and Robert Zemsky, "Cost Containment: Committing to a New Economic Reality," *Change* (November/December 1990): 20.

trolled, the resulting reduction of the number of government employees will benefit higher education.

In addition to government-imposed positions, higher education itself has been liberal in developing (1) staff positions to assist line operation managers; (2) new positions to fill required functions without determining whether the positions constitute 35-40 hours of productive work; (3) private secretarial support for administrators who use personal computers; (4) low-paying appointments at all levels that engender a lack of creativity and low productivity; (5) excessive levels of management and supervision; and (6) excessive decentralization of common functions such as admissions, registration, and financial aid.

Inexperienced and Untrained Management Personnel

Government is usually managed by lawyers, law firms by lawyers, hospitals by physicians, and higher education by professors. One common thread linking these four human endeavors is lack of professional management and good business practice. Another common thread is low productivity, which has put unrealistic financial pressure on our citizens to pay for education, medical attention, legal protection, and government services. Either the doctors, lawyers, and professors who want to manage social not-for-profit businesses have to be trained in management or gain experience in business, or their appointments have to be complemented by senior officers with business experience.

Personnel Fringe Benefits

Fringe benefits granted employees in higher education are often high, probably in part to offset the fact that there is no way of rewarding management or faculty for performance with profit sharing or ownership. As a result, contributions to retirement programs are generous. Administrative personnel enjoy a short workweek relative to industry and commonly one month's vacation, as well as many holidays, Christmas shutdowns, and quiet summers. The latter are a particularly troublesome aspect of managing employees who support academics and student affairs because the institution's productivity is limited during the "farming" (summer) season.

In addition to these conditions, higher education, as with industry, has suffered extraordinary increases in health insurance because the medical industry, as a result of its own poor management, is having great difficulty controlling costs.

Information Services

The use of computers and other electronic communication systems has expanded exponentially in higher education, as in society as a whole, during the past 25 years. To compete, higher education responded to the surging demand for computers and other electronic communication systems both at the academic level for instruction and at the administrative level to manage its business.[5] Higher education had to respond to this cost pressure and will continue to do so as electronic communications continue to expand. Electronic communications will consume an even greater percentage of total costs, requiring proper controls.

Cost Analysis

If higher education is not regarded as a business, it follows that only limited business procedures are in place. Fortunately, most institutions have established departmental operating budgets in response to the demographic problem and the cost pressures, but many are still lacking in these techniques. Unfortunately, many institutions with budget procedures in place conduct their budgetary affairs in the same manner as government organizations, not as businesses. For example, funds are spent as budgeted for fear of losing the funds, rather than saved and reserved for common need at a later date.[6]

Higher education lacks cost systems that identify revenue and margin by school, college, discipline, program, etc. It is difficult enough to control a business that is growing without proper cost analysis, let alone attempt to retrench a business without knowing what parts of the business make or lose money.[7]

In addition, a lack of costing and pricing experience made higher education vulnerable to the absorption of new or expanded programs. Without knowledge of cost factors, institutions have indulged in heavy tuition discounting for financial aid, generous tuition remission programs for employees and their families, expanded research programs, planned giving endowments that extend into a second-generation life expectancy, and idle plant/staff capacity during summer months. It is assumed that basic costs have been absorbed by "someone" and that the programs listed impose only a nominal cost to support. Proper pricing for these efforts have, therefore, been minimal or nonexistent.

---

[5]Richard E. Anderson and Joel W. Meyerson, eds., *Financing Higher Education in a Global Economy* (New York: American Council on Education and Macmillan Publishing Company, 1990), 66-67.

[6]Joseph Froomkin, ed., *The Crisis in Higher Education* (Montpelier, VT: City Press, 1983), 136.

[7]Daniel T. Layzell and Jan W. Lyddon, *Budgeting for Higher Education at the State Level: Enigma, Paradox, and Ritual*. ASHE-ERIC Higher Education Report no. 4 (Washington, DC: The George Washington University, 1990), 63-64.

As institutions downsize to address enrollment reductions, or to recapture a quality student body, the incrementally cost/priced nonacademic programs will become a greater portion of the business base. The cost pressure on the industry of higher education will be dramatic, and without dependable cost systems in place, management will fly blind.

Insurance

Insurance costs for higher education for protection of assets, general liability, and medical coverage are particularly problematic because higher education is labor-intensive and has an extraordinary amount of physical plant relative to its revenues. Insurance in all businesses has increased steadily during the past 15 years, but it has particularly driven up higher education costs because of the industry's intense people/facilities exposure.

Transfer of Operation Excesses to Quasi-Endowment

Contrary to popular belief, most not-for-profit organizations do not operate at break-even nor incur deficits. A business would quickly cease to exist if it incurred deficits. As a matter of fact, until recently, most not-for-profit institutions realized excesses of revenue from operations. Excesses are diverted to facility construction, financial aid, other programs requiring extraordinary expenditures, and transfers to quasi-endowments.

Unfortunately, higher education management discovered, particularly in the 1980s, that it was easy to increase tuition rates, spend a comfortable amount of money to operate the institution, and divert excesses into quasi-endowment. This approach to managing a business allowed the administration and the board of trustees to avoid two difficult tasks: (1) raising third-party funds for endowments and annual giving to subsidize current operations; and (2) controlling spending.

PHYSICAL PLANT PROBLEMS

Excess Capacity

Excess capacity is developing as a result of two causes: (1) declining student demographics; and (2) motivation from a marketing standpoint for institutions to expand their facilities and amenities to address a more competitive marketplace. For a period of time, the development of excess capacity in the residence facilities was delayed because, although there was a shrinking number of students attending institutions of higher education, more of them were demanding on-campus housing. This demand for housing has been addressed, and now the shrinking student body will finally create excess capacity in that sector at many institutions. In addition, there will be excess classroom, office, athletic/recreation, and parking facilities.

Energy Costs

Energy costs started their upward spiral during the first oil embargo in the early 1970s. Higher education suffered disproportionately to other businesses because of its people/facility concentration, which requires energy 24 hours a day, 7 days a week. With escalating energy costs comes the need for energy conservation methods, energy management systems, improved building structure and heat, ventilation and air conditioning (HVAC) design, and, ultimately, a resolve by the American public to gain energy independence from the Persian Gulf.

Deferred Maintenance

For the past 20 years, higher education has allowed its physical plant to fall into disrepair, resulting in an extraordinary backlog of deferred maintenance. Approximately $25 billion of deferred maintenance must be addressed immediately for functional/safety reasons, and another $50 billion of deferred maintenance should be addressed as soon as possible to restore the physical plant of the nation's institutions. When the going gets tough, facility maintenance is the first expenditure to be curtailed.

Although institutions have not made a serious attempt to reduce the deferred maintenance inventory in recent years, spending for normal preventive and corrective maintenance has been increased to prevent further slippage. To curtail corrective and restorative maintenance again and add to the $75 billion problem would be a disaster.

SOCIETAL CHANGES

Growth in Society's Standard of Living

The standard of living in the U.S. continued to rise with the advent of the dual-income family. The parents of college-age young people and the students themselves demanded more amenities and better living conditions commensurate with what they had come to expect at home. These demands are reflected in costs associated with operating the institutions. Note that this is one cost pressure in higher education that is not under the control of management. If the public wants to assist in achieving affordable tuition, they and their children will have to lower their standard of living for students attending college.

It is important to understand that although the family standard of living continued to improve, the family median income did not increase as rapidly during the 1980s as tuition increases.

Financial Aid

Financial aid is derived from many sources and takes form as either debt or an outright gift. The form of financial aid that affects tuition rates directly is the discounting of tuition to provide internal grants for financial aid from the institution itself. It is referred to as a "Robin Hood" program in that full tuition payers subsidize the needy. Tuition rates are increased in general to provide tuition forgiveness to the needy and to targeted constituencies, thus placing the wealthy in a position of paying a higher rate to provide more internal funds for those who will be granted a financial subsidy.

During the 1980s, institutions were pressed to increase the proportion of internal discounting in response to reductions in financial aid from the states and from the federal government, and to offset the extraordinary increases in tuition. Greater discounts created higher tuition rates and reduced the number of families "Robin Hood" could take from while increasing the number he had to support. Obviously, the mounting demand for financial aid and tuition discounting can be stabilized if costs are controlled and tuition is maintained at a reasonable level.

It appears that many institutions are increasing their discounts at a greater rate than they can increase their tuition. This will transfer the "subsidy" from the wealthy student to the institution and eventually result in deficit spending.

The Resident Experience

Along with the demands on higher education for a higher standard of living, the American public is defining the higher education years as a total life experience with room and board as part of the package. Although residence does not place pressure on tuition for an education, it adds to the total cost of higher education and is another area where the American public will have to work with higher education if there is a genuine desire to reduce total costs for a college degree.

Growth of Physical Activities Within Our Society

President Kennedy's exhortation for society to be more physically active and the disclosure through research that physical activity extends life while providing for improved general well-being have placed tremendous demands on higher education to increase the number of recreational and athletic facilities on campus. Recreational facilities provided today far exceed those provided for past generations. Multiple pools, weight rooms, dance studios, basketball courts, and practice fields abound. The situation has also been exacerbated by the fact that a much greater proportion of the students are now in residence and their primary recreational and physical activities are the responsibility of the institution. Again, this is an area where society has demanded programs that have a direct impact on the cost of higher education.

Inflation

Inflation in the late 1970s and early 1980s was unprecedented. It was coincidental and also unfortunate that the beginning of the demographic problem facing higher education in 1979 was also the beginning of an extraordinary inflation period for the years 1979 through 1983. Although inflation has abated in recent years, higher education has justified continued large tuition increases with the excuse that they had a catch-up situation regarding salaries and continuing inflation problems "unique" to education.

With this chapter, the stage has been set to address the problem at hand: what should be done to improve management of higher education, significantly reduce its cost demands, improve productivity, and realize affordable tuition rates.

PART

II

··········

Organization and Management

CHAPTER 2

The Board of Trustees and Chairperson

The first organization issue of any business entity is to establish a ruling body. In most for-profit and all not-for-profit organizations, the ruling body is a board. The not-for-profit board has the same basic responsibilities as a board of directors of a for-profit operation. However, board members are called trustees rather than directors because no individual or organization owns the assets of the institution, and board members must maintain the assets and funds in trust. This is a significant difference in responsibility of the members of the board. In a for-profit organization, the directors are representatives of the owners of the organization, who are stockholders. The only exception to this would be a sole proprietorship where the owner of the business chooses to govern with the assistance of a board, which consists of paid members of the firm.

Board members of a for-profit organization not only represent the stockholders but usually are expected to own a block of shares in their own name. It is also common practice to pay these members of the board for their services. Members of a not-for-profit institution serve to protect existing assets and contribute to the financial needs of the organization. Payment for their services would be inconsistent because theirs is a public trust and a public giving.

RESPONSIBILITIES OF THE BOARD OF TRUSTEES

Unencumbered revenues and assets in a not-for-profit institution of higher education are derived from two primary sources: education-related activities and restricted and unrestricted gifts. Because of this duality, the board of trustees also has the twofold responsibility of presiding over what is, for all intents and purposes, a business and raising funds to subsidize operations and accumulate capital.

Boards of trustees, unlike boards of directors, are usually composed of a large body of people, as many as 30 to 40. As is true of any organization, the larger the governing body, the more cumbersome it is to govern. The purpose of a large board in education is to broaden the fund-raising potential of the organization. Ideally, individuals who have one or more of the following attributes provide for a strong organization: (1) management expertise and experience; (2) independent wealth and a willingness to pass on a portion of it to the institution; (3) access to a network of wealthy individuals and foundations that could be cultivated to give to the institution, and (4) academic credentials with management experience in another institution of higher education.

Unfortunately, in higher education, a well-worn phrase in defining a trustee is "to give, get, or get off." This attitude excludes two other important attributes of an ideal member: academic and/or management experience. It should be understood by any individual who accepts an invitation to join a board of trustees that he or she will be expected to give to the organization. Theirs is a public trust, and their motivating reason for joining a board should be to serve society by helping to sustain a social entity. For want of a better formula, I would recommend that 25 percent of the members of a board be wealthy individuals who are willing to give to the institution and 25 percent be those who have access to wealthy individuals, management experience, or academic credentials. A more positive statement regarding the attributes of an ideal board member is "give, get, and guide."

The primary responsibility of the board of trustees and the chairperson is the appointment, monitoring, and appropriate rewarding of the chief officer of the institution.[1] As is true for any business organization, the chief officer is the cornerstone upon which a successful institution is built. In addition to being the leader and manager of the organization, the chief officer must have the vision to successfully guide the organization for the next five to ten years. This condition is particularly true today because of the changing demographics that have adversely affected enrollments for the past 17 years and will continue to plague higher education to the end of the century. The complicated specifications for a chief officer, particularly in these troubled times, are reviewed in the next chapter.

---

[1]Barbara E. Taylor, *Working Effectively with Trustees: Building Cooperative Campus Leadership*, ASHE-ERIC Higher Education Report no. 2 (Washington, DC: Association for the Study of Higher Education, 1987), 31.

Other responsibilities of the board, similar to the board of directors of a for-profit organization, are developing policy for overview and guidance of the organization and long-range strategic planning. Responsibilities that are unique to the not-for-profit sector are the fund-raising requirements, mentioned earlier, and the growth of those funds through careful investing.

I have always had difficulty separating policy from long-range planning because it is a catch-22. It is difficult for a board to develop comprehensive policy for governance of the institution if the institution has not developed a long-term strategy. Basic policy for day-to-day governance can be developed without a long-term plan. However, those policies that will protect the organization from foolish changes in direction or the frivolous spending of money are difficult to develop without a plan to provide management with the flexibility it needs to make strategic changes in direction. In later chapters, we will review long-range strategic planning and its integration with annual operating budgets.

COMMITTEES OF THE BOARD

A board of trustees addresses its business through an assortment of standing committees. Primary committees consist of academics, business and finance, investments, student affairs, and institutional advancement (primarily fund raising). Usually these functions are overseen by officers designated as vice presidents. The respective vice presidents in turn report to the chair of their respective committees. In recent years, sub-committees have also been formed at many institutions to preside over the use of computers and enroll-ment management. In addition, trustees sometimes use compensation com-mittees to review their officers' remuneration packages. Standing committees are presided over by an executive committee, which includes the chairperson of the board, vice chairperson, the chairpersons of the individual standing committees, and, in many cases, at-large members.

An interrelationship exists between standing committees: for example, if a board of trustees is large enough, which is frequently true in higher education, members of the board will serve on more than one committee. The many members and many committees offer the opportunity for appropriate cross-memberships. For instance, the chairpersons of the business and finance committee and the investment committee could be members of each other's committee, as well as the committee over which they preside as chairperson.

From an operations point of view, the primary trustee committee is the academic committee because academics is the business of higher education. A unique feature of higher education is that students are both the customer and the product of the business. The institution is marketed to the student at the time of admission, and four years later upon graduation, the student becomes the product of the business. This dual role within higher education only serves to make the business complicated, different, interesting, and, if carefully managed, challenging.

The role of the academic division in setting the instructional plans and aspirations of the institution is paramount; for this reason, the academic committee is the primary committee of the board. The direction of academics must be in place before the other standing committees can play their supporting roles. Once the academics mission is established, the next standing committee that falls into sequence is student affairs. When the student body is defined, it is the responsibility of the student affairs committee to address their housing, health, counseling, and other needs. In addition, recreational programs are required to support both residential and commuting students.

After the academic and student affairs committees have outlined their plans, and general direction has been provided by management and the board of trustees, the role of the business and finance committee is to develop the operational and financial structure to accomplish these endeavors. The business and finance committee must be aware of all activities within the academic and student affairs committees in order to determine the financial resources required to house the activities and control the expenditures against operating budgets. In addition to operating budgets, the business and finance committee will serve as the focal point for long-term strategic plans to determine revenue and expenditure flows that will enable the organization to remain solvent. The business and finance committee should work hand in glove with the institutional advancement committee to determine a comprehensive revenue flow including third-party giving as an overall business package. The importance of the institutional advancement committee is in direct relationship to that organization's success in raising money. Without a strong fund-raising component, the business and finance committee will find itself overly dependent on the primary sources of revenues for operating an institution—tuition and fees.

The remaining standing committee is investment. The funds represented by endowments, fund balances, and working capital must be invested in various securities and managed by the investment committee. The role of this committee is reviewed in detail in Chapter 10. It is important to note that the business and finance committee must be informed of expected revenues to be derived from the earnings on endowment investments, and the indirect support that can be provided the institution from continued endowments accumulation and equipment/facility gifts.

As mentioned earlier, three other committees take on significance: computer information services, enrollment management, and officer compensation. Of the three, the most significant is information services, which oversees the use of computers in administration and academics. If the role of the computer has been deemed to be important enough and a vice presidency has been set up for this area, a standing committee should be established. Computer support is becoming an increasingly important business consideration for the board because spending on computer support can consume as much as five to ten percent of gross annual revenues.[2]

Although many boards are establishing enrollment management committees and designating a vice president with specific responsibilities for marketing, it is possibly a temporary phenomenon. Serious marketing is new to higher education, and during the remainder of the 1990s it will be defined and appropriately financed. Ultimately, it will assume its appropriate place in the organization; at that point the need for interim concentrated attention of the board should cease to exist.

Although not an operating committee, the officer compensation committee of the board of trustees is becoming increasingly important because the management of higher education is becoming more complicated. Executive remuneration in higher education is a difficult area to address because the business is owned by no one, and therefore there are no stockholders. For this reason, it is impossible to reward officers with ownership. Their sole source of income is either in the form of immediate remuneration or deferred income. Fortunately, the government has been generous in its approach to tax-deferred income for people in the education field. As higher education business problems worsen during the 1990s and because it is impossible to offer opportunities to accumulate wealth through ownership, it is going to be difficult for higher education to attract and retain good business managers who can handle a highly competitive marketplace.

The standing committees, with the exception of the officer compensation committee, should meet two or three times a year prior to meetings of the full board. The executive committee should meet before the board and provide an opportunity for the chairpersons of the individual standing committees to gather and review their concerted efforts, as well as the financial ramifications of their aspirations. If the chairpersons of the standing committees are communicating and linking their activities appropriately, in concert with the chairperson of the board, the final position on all matters presented to the full board will usually be a formality.

Most businesses operate within a formal organization, usually the traditional pyramid with one individual, a chief officer, at the top supported by various officers and the department heads, directors, and deans. Again we are faced with a duality in higher education. The chief officer, who is the president or chancellor, is not always the best individual to handle day-to-day

---

[2]Brian L. Hawkins, "Preparing for the Next Wave of Computers on Campus," *Change* (January/February 1991): 24-31.

operations. Frequently, in higher education the chief officer is selected because of his or her academic strengths, his or her vision for an academic organization, and/or his or her ability to raise funds. Lacking may be the ability to manage a troubled, complicated financial entity in a turbulent marketplace.

RESPONSIBILITIES OF THE CHAIRPERSON

The number-one person on the board of trustees is the chairperson. This individual presides over board and executive committee meetings and usually is invited to attend standing committee meetings. The chairperson's most important responsibility is to oversee the proper selection of the chief officer for the institution and to determine when that individual should step down, resign, retire, or be terminated, if such drastic action is necessary.

Colleges and universities often attempt to fill the chairperson position with a graduate of the institution, believing that a graduate will feel a sense of dedication to the organization and possibly will be generous in his or her own giving to the institution. Although the chief officer should take the lead as the individual responsible for fund raising, the chairperson should organize fund raising consistent with the strategic plan and be the lightning rod for attracting funds, particularly among trustees.

The chairperson must be a leader. A large board of 30 to 40 members that only meets two to four times a year requires careful coordination to develop the agendas of the standing committees to achieve their missions, and to ensure close coordination between the chairs of the subcommittees and the officers of the institution.

The chairperson is responsible for developing the policies that will govern management of the institution through the board of trustees, the chief officer of the institution, and the vice presidents. Like all officers, chairpersons are elected to a one-year term at the annual meeting. A good chairperson should remain in office long enough to realize the development and fulfillment of his or her initiatives. No organization needs a dynasty, however. It would be wise to limit the tenure of the chairperson to five years.

Three suggestions for success as a chairperson are (1) be closely attuned to the internal activities and the effectiveness of the chief officer; (2) have the ability to ask the right questions of all officers responsible for running the institution; and (3) insist that the institution be guided by long-term strategic plans.

FOR FURTHER READING

Fisher, James L. *The Board and the President.* American Council on Education/Oryx Press Series on Higher Education. Phoenix, AZ: Oryx Press, 1991.

Ingram, Richard T., et al. *The Handbook of College and University Trusteeship.* San Francisco: Jossey-Bass, 1980.

CHAPTER

The Chief Officer

Higher education did not evolve as a business[1] but as a collection of learned scholars and teachers. For this reason higher education institutions did not develop the precise structure of a business with clear definitions for a chief executive officer, chief operating officer, and chief academic officer. This chapter will review the various organizational structures that can be used to fulfill management responsibilities for the central direction of higher education. The different models can be tailored to the talents of incumbents, the size and structure of the institution, the profile for an individual search, and the will of the board of trustees.

The board of trustees will appoint an individual to be the chief officer of the institution and grant that individual the title of president (for a college) or chancellor (for a network of colleges organized as a university at various campuses). The office of the president is the most critical position to be defined in an organization. It requires a carefully detailed job description of responsibilities and positions reporting to the office.

Frequently, a job description for the office of the president evolves from the position profile that was developed by the board of trustees at the time a search was initiated for a new president. A changing of the guard is an opportunity to redirect and restructure an institution to cope with current problems and strike off in a new strategic direction. Times change and skill requirements change as well.

Before the job description for the president can be defined, it is necessary to reevaluate all major responsibilities assigned to the president's office to deter-

---

[1]Donald E. Walker, *The Effective Administrator: A Practical Approach to Problem Solving, Decision Making, and Campus Leadership* (San Francisco: Jossey-Bass, Inc., 1979), 10.

mine whether they should be vested with the new president or assigned to another officer in the organization. The primary responsibilities for consideration are the following:

- executive officer
- operating officer
- planning strategist
- academic officer
- primary fund raiser

The presidency should include chief executive officer responsibility. The very title of chief executive marks the individual as the lead officer in the organization, a responsibility that should not be delegated to another executive.

The chief operating officer is the individual who oversees day-to-day operations and serves as the point person for most executive decisions. All other officers should report to this individual. The chief operating officer can be an individual reporting to the president, or this position can remain with the chief officer if the organization is not large or the chief officer enjoys and possesses the time and talent to execute day-to-day operations. A separation of chief executive and chief operating responsibilities is cumbersome and usually adds staff, cost, and operational delays. However, the chief operating officer position is appropriate in large organizations, such as a university, and the title given is frequently executive vice president.

The planning strategist is the individual in the organization who has the vision of his or her institution's role in society and how the organization currently fills that role. Ideally, primary planning responsibilities should be retained by the president (chief officer) or the executive vice president (chief operating officer).

The planning strategist cannot afford to commit an institution to a rigid planning sequence because the external world changes continuously and so should the institution. In Chapters 4 and 5 on strategic long-term planning and operating budgets, we will review many reasons why a planning strategist has to be retained by the president. This position is becoming more important to higher education because of the combination of competitive marketing conditions and tuition costs that are becoming too high to be compatible with the best interests of society and the continued economic development of the country.

The responsibility for planning strategy can remain with the president or be assigned to another officer, possibly the vice president for academics or the provost, or the chief business officer. If planning strategist responsibilities are delegated to the provost or business officer, that position should have status over the other officers for developing direction and formulating marketing and policy change. Unless there is a separation of chief executive and chief operating responsibilities, it would not be wise to delegate primary planning responsibilities to an individual who does not possess a "second in command" position.

The planning responsibility for academic development of the institution can reside with the president, but more commonly it will be assigned to the vice president of academic affairs, or the provost.

The last responsibility for review under the chief officer is that of being primary fund raiser. Fund raising is an executive responsibility that is unique to the not-for-profit sector of the business world. Fund raising in higher education requires third-party monies provided by individuals, foundations, governments, and, in some cases, industry.

The day-to-day operation of raising funds and administrating an alumni program is vested with the vice president for institutional affairs through the development office. Although the president may delegate operating responsibility for fund raising to that officer, it is not in the best interest of the institution to allow the president to sidestep fund raising simply because he or she does not enjoy asking for money. Further, if the president opts not to participate in the cultivation phase of fund raising, and wishes to serve only as primary "closer," it will seriously hamper development of a successful fund raising program and alienate alumni. Major givers are going to expect to receive a certain amount of attention from the president while being cultivated for a major gift for a specific need of the institution. The benefactors will want to know the individual who runs the institution and how he or she feels about the need for a particular gift. They have every right to expect the warm attention of the person who is in charge. It usually will fall upon the president to be the individual who makes the closing and shakes hands on the arrangement. As is said in many areas of responsibility, "It goes with the turf."

CHOOSING THE CHIEF OFFICER

Figures 3.1, 3.2, 3.3, and 3.4 display organization charts that show various options for organizing the office of the president and the major responsibilities discussed so far in this chapter. In all instances, it is understood that primary fund raising resides with the chief officer. Organization A (described in Figure 3.1) is the most common arrangement for responsibilities assigned to the chief officer. Organizations B and C (see Figures 3.2 and 3.3) present possible options for an inside/outside approach to governance if there are extenuating circumstances.

Chief officers in higher education frequently lack management training and, in many cases, achieve their high position without benefit of any management experience. In the past, a growing student population provided an expanding revenue base, and costs were relatively low and stable. In that environment, the president could operate relatively successfully without for-

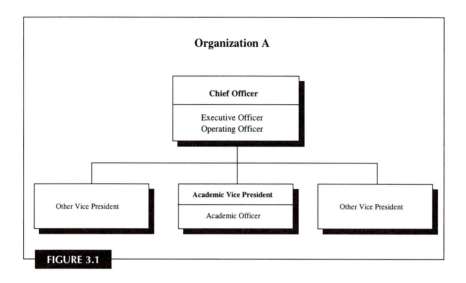

FIGURE 3.1

mal training or experience because a level of inefficiency could be afforded. In today's highly competitive market, however, it is essential that a president be appointed who has successfully performed on a management team as president, or at least as a vice president. Other worthy candidates include academicians with management experience who have acquired an MBA before assuming the responsibilities of a chief officer, or individuals with management experience and a doctorate in some field.

It is not enough for the chief officer to have an understanding of the various departments and functions of an institution. The individual should have an intimate knowledge of how the various functions interrelate, are dependent on each other, and support the whole of the institution. Without this knowledge it would be difficult to preside over a complicated business, manage operating budgets, and successfully participate in market and financial strategic long-term planning.

A president should be selected for a particular time in the development of an institution. All organizations go through stages of development or deterioration; the selection of a president is an opportunity to redirect an institution and address current needs. This is why it is so important that the board of trustees gives adequate thought to the development of a profile for an individual to succeed the incumbent. A candidate with the basic strengths desired can always be supplemented and complemented by the strengths and talents of existing officers, or selected changes in the organization can be made to achieve the whole desired.

The chief officer will be the primary funnel through which the position of the administration on various issues is postured. The chief officer makes the final decisions on all matters of importance that go to the board, and it is the

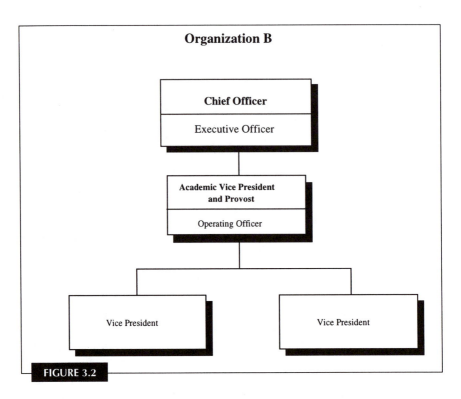

FIGURE 3.2

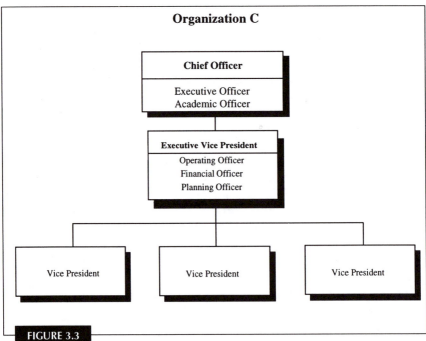

FIGURE 3.3

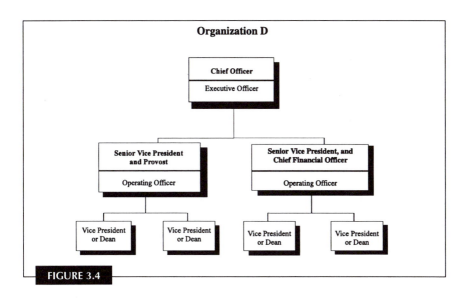

Organization D

Chief Officer
Executive Officer

Senior Vice President and Provost
Operating Officer

Senior Vice President, and Chief Financial Officer
Operating Officer

Vice President or Dean

Vice President or Dean

Vice President or Dean

Vice President or Dean

FIGURE 3.4

role of the other officers to support that position once the chief officer makes a determination. For these reasons, the chief officer will be the focal point of power and should possess the management ability to improve upon the institution during his or her incumbency.

The power vested in the chief officer is necessary. However, the board should be ever alert to information contained in management reports and comments made by other officers in the organization warning of unfolding events that are not in the best interest of the institution. The board fulfills the difficult position of selecting and supporting the chief officer but must be tuned to weaknesses that could hurt the institution. Many chief officers fail, some lose interest, and many find events outpacing their abilities to continue to manage successfully. As was discussed in the previous chapter, the most important responsibilities of the board are to appoint a chief officer, monitor the performance of that individual, determine when it is time for a change, and preside over an orderly management transition.

Higher education is increasingly becoming involved in problems beyond the campus.

- Cost containment has become critical because median family income is not rising as fast as the cost of higher education.
- Marketing has gained importance because of the student demographic problem.
- Fund raising has gained importance because of increased financial pressure on higher education.

- Involvement in the unfolding international marketplace requires knowledge of what is happening, contacts, and networking.
- Strategic long-term planning has gained importance because of the above four items and requires more contact with outside individuals, other institutions, the government, and industry.

Higher education will evolve through a period in which chief officers with successful professional management experience in dealing with a highly competitive marketplace and limited financial resources will be difficult to identify. Formulating the office of the president may require broader use of other management models. There may be an interim need for dual roles whereby two or three individuals share primary responsibilities.

A possible consideration would be a separation of responsibilities or an "inside/outside" relationship. In this model, the outside officer should be the gregarious visionary who (1) is interested in developing a wide group of friends, colleagues, and contacts; (2) sincerely enjoys raising money; (3) has an interest in the development of strategic planning of the organization's future; and (4) has the ability to formulate a marketing program and institute that program throughout the institution's marketplace. This individual can be supported by an inside executive with responsibilities for day-to-day operation of the institution and successful execution of activities within the operating budget/plan. Figures 3.2 and 3.3 present examples that offer the opportunity for an inside/outside management concept.

Figure 3.4 shows a fourth organization option. This is the division of the institution into two senior vice presidencies reporting to the chief office. In this organization, academic operations are placed under a senior vice president and provost, and business operations report to a senior vice president and chief financial officer. Many institutions already use this model. In some organizations, it is formalized with the various vice presidents reporting to the senior vice presidents, and in other organizations it functions as a troika without formal structure. However, formal organizations function more smoothly than informal ones.

THE IMPORTANCE OF SUBORDINATE OFFICERS

Specifying and selecting an appropriate chief officer for an institution is only the first step in the development of a management arrangement. No matter how strong a chief officer is, he or she can not be effective unless supported by capable subordinate officers—"Nobody can lead the band and play all the instruments." There is a lot of truth to the statement that good subordinates make a superior look good. Any chief officer who does not retain the very best will not serve the institution well.

The importance of subordinate officers brings up another subject regarding the future management of higher education. If we accept the premise that higher education is in a highly competitive environment and should be run like a business, it is necessary for the chief officer to demand a compensation program that supports development of a strong management team.

Officer remuneration is hamstrung by the not-for-profit designation assigned to higher education. The strongest motivating feature of a remuneration package for executives in the for-profit sector is the opportunity to participate in the business, "to have a piece of the action." The harder they work and the more successful they are, the more they will earn in the form of a percentage of profits or the granting of stock options that will allow them to participate in the growth and development of the business. In higher education, officers are limited to base salary, the growth of pension programs through advantageous deferred compensation programs, the limited use of bonuses, and the usual perks of automobiles, expense accounts, club memberships, and, in some cases, institution housing. (It should be noted that institution housing has been a mixed blessing since World War II because many executives in higher education lost the opportunity for the extraordinary capital gains that have been realized in housing during the past 50 years.)

If the board of trustees agrees that it takes a strong support team to ensure expected performance by the chief officer, then it follows that the board should take as much interest in the compensation packages of the vice presidents as in that of the chief officer.

Although options are limited, higher education still has two strong remuneration opportunities.

- Deferred compensation sums to be accumulated for retirement
- A well-defined bonus program

Officers in not-for-profit organizations are frequently neither rewarded nor chastised for their performance.[2] Goals and performance factors have been considered to be too difficult, if not impossible, to define because of the not-for-profit and social-serving features of the business. However, if the reader accepts the fact that higher education is a business, then there are many performance criteria that can be developed against which the officers can be measured, rewarded, and judged. Organizations with well-developed strategic long-term plans, coupled with annual operating budgets, offer performance factors that are quantified or have sufficient description to define reward criteria. Select those factors that are important to the development and success of the institution and delegate the objectives to the operating officers for execution.

---

[2]James L. Fisher, *The Board and the President* (Phoenix, AZ: Oryx Press, 1991), 73.

Assuming that all candidates for a chief officer position are educated, experienced, and appear to be well suited to the institution's current needs, the primary characteristics of the individual selected will be a proven record of leadership combined with a solid vision of where the business should be directed. The 1990s are witnessing a change in delivery of education in terms of quality and productivity. The selection of chief officers, the restructuring of the organization to complement their management style, and the development of an officer cadre will determine which institutions of higher education will be online for the new century.

FOR FURTHER READING

Bensimen, Estela M.; Neumann, Anna; and Birnbaum, Robert. *Making Sense of Administrative Leadership: The "L" Word in Higher Education.* ASHE-ERIC Higher Education Report no. 1. Washington, DC: School of Education and Human Development, The George Washington University, 1989.

Fisher, James L. *The Board and the President.* American Council on Education/Oryx Press Series on Higher Education. Phoenix, AZ: Oryx Press, 1991.

Fisher, James L.; Tack, Martha W.; and Wheeler, Karen J. *The Effective College President.* American Council on Education/Oryx Press Series on Higher Education. Phoenix, AZ: Oryx Press, 1988.

Plante, Patricia R., with Robert L. Caret. *Myths and Realities of Academic Administration.* American Council on Education/Oryx Press Series on Higher Education. Phoenix, AZ: Oryx Press, 1990.

Walker, Donald F. *The Effective Administrator: A Practical Approach to Problem Solving, Decision Making, and Campus Leadership.* San Francisco: Jossey-Bass, Inc., 1979.

PART

III

·········

Strategic
Overview

CHAPTER 4

Strategic Long-Term Planning

S trategic planning has become an important issue in higher education during the past 10 years. After 350 years of uninterrupted growth in population in combination with an increasing number of young people interested in higher education, the pattern changed in 1979. A declining birth rate, which had commenced 18 years earlier, finally caught up with higher education. Fortunately for higher education, there was a reprieve as a result of the women's movement, which began in earnest in the 1960s. As women considered careers as a life option, they realized the need for a college degree, and in increasing numbers through the early 1980s, they pursued higher education and eventually slightly surpassed the enrollment of males.[1] In combination with this phenomenon, more young people opted for higher education than in the past as funds become available due to the evolution of the two-income family.

With women fully participating in the higher education experience, institutions of higher learning are now experiencing the full demographic impact of declining numbers of potential students. Colleges are faced with a marketplace that will continue to decline through the mid 1990s. Institutions will compete to maintain the quality of their student body without decreasing enrollment and losing revenues.

In addition to the women's movement, a second phenomenon delayed the financial impact of declining demographics: the extraordinary demand for campus housing. More students, supported by their parents, wished to fully experience higher education by living on campus. This was a fortuitous trend

---

[1]National Center for Education Statistics, *Projections of Higher Education Statistics to 2002*, (Washington, DC: U.S. Department of Education, Office of Educational Research and Improvement, NCES 91-490, 1991), 28.

because room and board offer an opportunity to realize significant operating margins. (Room and board as a revenue source is reviewed in detail in Chapter 8.) Most recently, wealthy international students who choose to live on campus have been aggressively recruited.

It now appears that all reprieves that delayed the impending reduction in revenues have been exhausted, and it is time for higher education to stop wearing out the word *strategic* and get down to serious planning for survival in a highly competitive environment.

Historically, long-range planning in higher education has centered around financial projections that were accommodated, over the last couple of decades, by the ability to handle massive amounts of numbers with the computer. The words that went with the music were, for the most part, dreams and aspirations rather than substantive marketing evaluation and strategic placement in a marketing niche that existed or was to be devised. To be strategic, long-range planning has to be market-oriented and has to contain alternatives to a market position that goes awry.

Educating people might seem like a simple endeavor, but in reality it is probably one of the most complicated business endeavors in the marketplace. There are many fields—education, business, liberal arts, law, medicine, etc.—and within these fields there are many directions that the student can take before earning a degree. Further complicating the marketing problem is the proliferation of institutions of higher education, about 3,400 individual institutions.[2] Within these institutions are universities that contain many colleges. As a result of this market condition, a phenomenon that probably will occur between now and the turn of the century is consolidation of institutions through mergers and, in some cases, the demise of institutions that cannot compete. If this does not occur, the public will face the need to support an industry with excess capacity. How does an institution acquire and develop a quality student body? How much success is the result of the institution's ability to attract a bright, highly motivated student who will probably succeed in life no matter from where he or she graduates? What kind of results can be expected from a first-rate faculty who are up-to-date in their field, have vision, and, most important, have the ability to motivate students and convey their knowledge to a group of individuals? Bridging these considerations is the development of a basic curriculum that is contemporary, visionary, and interrelates well with all other course activity within the institution, particularly the professional fields.

---

[2]Charles J. Anderson, Deborah J. Carter, and Andrew G. Malizic, *1989-1990 Fact Book on Higher Education* (Phoenix, AZ: Oryx Press, 1989), 33.

DEVELOPING A STRATEGIC LONG-TERM PLAN

With the above questions defining a problem that requires a solution, let's start by outlining the orderly steps to develop an institutional strategic long-term plan. For conceptual purposes, the outline will restrict itself to development of a strategic plan for a single college rather than a university, which has the added complication of multiple markets and allocation of the university's resources between colleges. Planning should follow a format such as the following:

- Update the mission statement and operation goals as conceived by management and the board of trustees
- Conduct a thorough review of the marketplace
- Conduct a comprehensive review of competing institutions
- Conduct an objective market review of how the student admission operations recruit
- Assess the strengths and weaknesses of the institution relative to the competition
- Develop a marketing strategy to posture the institution where it wishes to be in the marketplace
- Develop a detailed academic plan to support marketing intentions
- Rewrite the mission statement and operation goals to conform to a planned new direction—if changed
- Change marketing, advertising, faculty, and curriculum to reposture in the marketplace
- Develop a market strategy with options
- Project enrollments and other revenue sources for the planned period
- Develop resource requirements for personnel, facilities, and revenues
- Prepare costing and pricing for academic programs, auxiliary enterprises, and other revenue activities
- Plan third-party giving programs and capital campaign requirements to support needs identified in the strategic plan
- Develop a financial resource flow model to support the plan
- Modify the strategic plan to provide balance between ambitions and realistic financial resource support
- Review the financial model and redo plans until financial equilibrium is achieved
- Update the strategic plan annually prior to preparation of operating budgets

Developing a mission statement and planned goals is probably the most difficult step in the preparation of a long-range plan. For those institutions that have never participated in long-range integrated planning, mission statements tend to be general, lofty sounding, full of hyperbole, and identical to those of many other institutions. In other words, they are an itemized list of "Motherhood Statements." Mission statements and operation goals will change with time. This is particularly true for those institutions that prepare a plan in which the strategy is to change their mission either subtly or significantly over a period of time.

An effective mission statement should contain a broad statement of strategy that provides policy direction to the management of the institution. If this is not done, then the mission statement, by nature, will take on the gist of general, lofty-sounding statements about what the institution is currently doing and the fact that it will do it better than anybody else. The mission statement should be brief and supported by specific goals, which will be changed periodically as they are accomplished, replaced, or abandoned. Properly written, the document will take the form of policy with separate specific operation goals concerning direction and approach.

THE MARKETING PLAN

Marketing in a competitive environment is new to the industry of higher education. Few institutions possess the in-house talent for comprehensive marketing evaluation. I recommend that a consultant with successful experience in higher education be retained for initial studies. Beware, however, of consultants who base their report and recommendations primarily on historical research—the 1990s are a new ball game. The consultant must have a track record as a visionary. Find a consultant who advised an institution five or ten years ago, envisioned today's market, and provided successful guidance.

The First Marketing Review

The first marketing review should evaluate how employers view the education quality of your graduates and the stature of those students as individuals compared to graduates from competing institutions. Included in the market survey should be sections on what aspects of your institution's education program employers appreciate and what changes they would recommend to provide graduates more appropriately educated to address problems of the contemporary world.

The marketplace should be reexamined periodically, particularly after changes are made to the curriculum to determine if the changes were appropriate. Curriculum is developed by professors who, for the most part, are scholars who lack the work experience that their students are going to be subjected to upon graduation. Continuous, constructive tension between the faculty and the marketplace is essential if an institution is going to maintain a building-block approach to development of a curriculum supported by faculty research that is relevant to society's needs. The gestation period from the time curriculum changes are perceived until they are instituted and reflected in graduates is recognized by industry as seven to ten years—minimum.

The Second Marketing Review

The second marketing review of competing institutions can be difficult. The competition is not knowingly going to provide information that will allow you to compete against them. Although you will know as much about their position in the marketplace as they do with a proper market survey, you will not know what their long-term strategy is. Therein lies the basis of key strategic positioning. If they are not doing strategic planning they will probably not make any changes, and you will know exactly how to posture yourself in the marketplace. Unfortunately, if they are doing a good job of planning, they might be making changes that will counter your moves or better them.

A review of strengths and weaknesses relative to the competition is difficult. First, a college must be entirely honest with itself, and second, identify strengths and weaknesses as a result of a market survey and other sources of information. The second problem is the old bugaboo—perception. How your institution is perceived in the real world is how your institution will be judged. In fact, you might find that your perception is quite different from the public's perception. If this is the case, then your marketing approach has to change in order to nourish proper perception.

Preview of strengths and weaknesses relative to the competition is also difficult because those institutions with which you compete for students today will, in all probability, change as a result of your strategic posturing. As an example, any institution that is going to make bold changes to improve the quality of its faculty, curriculum, and plant is going to increase costs, which will increase price. Price will have a major impact—you will be too expensive for many of your old customer group, and improved quality probably will not be apparent to the targeted customer group for an extended period of time. Improved quality will be noticed, and a different customer group will evolve—eventually.

The Third Marketing Review

The third marketing review is an investigation of the methods used by the admissions office to recruit students. This review will include the perceived market, how the market is addressed, timing of the various activities, and the quality and effectiveness of the admissions staff.

An integral part of the recruitment review is the coordination of financial aid with recruitment for the purpose of maximizing desired quality of the student body in concert with achieving the planned student profile.

Supported by two thorough market evaluations prepared by a competent consulting firm(s), in combination with an honest assessment of strengths and weaknesses relative to the competition, the administration can reconfigure the institution's programs and mission to be consistent with what has been learned relative to what is planned. Finally, develop a marketing strategy for future years, perhaps the institution's first genuine strategic approach to the marketplace.

Many aspects of your organization may have to change: curriculum, emphasis between disciplines within a field, type of faculty, admissions policies regarding type of students and their whereabouts, and, certainly, image as related to publicity, marketing, and admissions. Key changes may be needed in two other areas as well: selected changes in management or organization, and, possibly, changes in the board of trustees and its leadership.

COSTING AND PRICING OF THE INSTITUTION

The next step in the development of a plan is the costing and pricing of the institution for the next five years. This exercise will be conducted with the use of a computer to handle all the data. It is also assumed at this point that the institutional research people have over the years done a good job of developing operating ratios required to make quick parametric adjustments for the development of financials.

With the use of business assumptions and appropriate indices, develop a revenue flow for the five-year period based on knowledge to date. Tuition and fees will probably continue to be the primary source of revenues, and therefore, enrollment projections based on the marketing plan will be especially critical. (Revenue sources other than tuition will be covered in the chapters of Part IV, which outline the many revenue opportunities available to an institution.)

After the basic plan has been accepted by the management team, it is a good idea to make selected changes in the assumptions used for developing revenues and costs and run "what if" exercises on the computer model to determine their sensitivity and impact on revenue flow and spending.

Many organizations find it easier to use constant dollars in preparing long-term financial computer simulations because estimating inflation and its impact on expenditures and revenue is impossible, and the escalating numbers cloud the dynamics of the planning strategies. Here's an example. The five-year projection of financial activity has disclosed that the institution will be incurring deficits commencing the third year. Management has already worked its "what if" exercises and satisfied themselves that the plan regarding specific programs is in balance and that the institution can probably be aggressive in tuition pricing to avoid a deficit.

In this example, it is determined that a 2 percent tuition increase in each of the final three years of the five-year plan would be appropriate. (See Figures

	MODEL YEARS				
Tuition Revenue	$ 10,000	$11,000	$12,000	$12,000	$12,000
Expenditures and Transfers	9,500	11,000	12,200	12,400	12,600
Expenditures (Over) Under Tuition Revenue	$ 500	$ -0-	$ (200)	$ (400)	$ (600)

PROJECTED TUITION DEFICITS OVER FIVE YEARS
FIGURE 4.1

	MODEL YEARS				
Tuition Revenue	$10,000	$11,000	$12,240	$12,484	$12,734
Expenditures and Transfers	9,500	11,000	12,200	12,400	12,600
Expenditures (Over) Under Tuition Revenue	$ 500	$ -0-	$ 40	$ 84	$ 134

PROJECTED TUITION INCREASES USING A 2 PERCENT FORMULA
FIGURE 4.2

4.1 and 4.2.) It is important to note that the two percentage points each year are in addition to whatever normal increase would be made in response to inflation and program add-ons. Therefore, if a normal increase for years 3, 4, and 5 will be 3 percent, 5 percent, and 4 percent, the planned rate need will be 5 percent, 7 percent, and 6 percent.

Next we will review sponsored research and its impact on the strategic plan. Sponsored research is extremely important to the quality development and recognition of an institution and, if properly handled, provides the appropriate linkage with industry and the government to keep an institution online with contemporary developments. Note, however, that sponsored research, particularly industry- and foundation-funded research, is heavily subsidized by tuition and therefore, the more aggressive an institution is in the development of its research program, the greater the pressure on tuition and the risk of pricing the institution out of the marketplace. The good news is that faculty members who can obtain such funding are obviously up-to-date in their discipline and how it applies to "real world" problems. The financial implications of sponsored research projects are reviewed in Chapter 6.

Invariably, the first summary of revenues against expenditures is going to disclose extraordinary deficits. It is human nature that plans become "wish lists," and everyone strives for excellence and a "number one" position, which is terribly expensive. Reality will evolve in the development of the plan as every aspect of it is thoroughly reviewed. Certain programs will have to be cut back or eliminated; other programs will have to be delayed. Perhaps some of the expenditures can be offset by new forms of revenue. The cycle at this point becomes one of devising changes, making reductions, and continually running the model until acceptable cash flow levels are achieved.

The development of financial resources other than tuition and fees involves the following steps:

- Determining the type and amount of research required to maintain a viable market position
- Determining what excesses can be achieved over the years and made available for immediate operating costs or deferral in quasi-endowment
- Determining the flow of operating funds from endowment earnings and unrestricted gifts for operations
- Determining income that can be realized on the investment of working capital
- Determining revenue opportunities extraneous to the college's mission, from both related and unrelated college events and business ventures
- Establishing margins that can be realized between the pricing of room and board and their respective cost
- Determining margin to be realized from the bookstore and other service operations
- Developing third-party giving sources from a capital campaign, if contemplated. (This is a closed-loop exercise, because a capital campaign requires a strategic plan to define needs and the plan requires the capital flow from the campaign.)

The financial model should be continually exercised until a balance is determined satisfactory to management and the board of trustees. Hopefully, "satisfactory" means that the institution will have a flow of excess funds for future reinvestment in the institution.

You now have a strategic long-term plan. The day you finish the plan and receive final approval is the day before you begin to develop your next five-year plan. A solid five-year strategic plan serves as the foundation for annual operating budgets. The annual exercise of updating the five-year plan should be completed before instructions go out for development of the following year's operating budget. Properly prepared, truncating the first year of a five-year plan provides definitive guidance for development of the operating budget. (Development of an integrated annual operating budget is covered in Chapter 5.)

THE MERGER OPTION

Before completing this chapter on planning, it would be inappropriate, considering today's circumstances, not to discuss the strategic option of mergers and acquisitions. Assuming an institution has an appropriate mission, a good program, and a service that is in demand, society and all of the constituencies associated with an institution in financial difficulty are best served by merger if the alternative is the eventual financial collapse and demise of the institution. Allowing an institution to fail financially and then have society pay for the start-up and development of a similar operation elsewhere is wasteful.

Perhaps education in this country has reached the point where it would be better served intellectually and financially by fewer independent institutions. Consolidation of institutions would reduce personnel, more appropriately use the existing facilities of the institutions, and make excess facilities available for sale or lease. Perhaps the time has come to accept that the halls of ivy do not necessarily have to be contained in one contiguous campus but could be located in various areas, much the same as industry finds its operating facilities diversely located.

Theoretically, mergers between institutions should be much less complicated than they are in industry. There are no stockholders. Therefore, there is no need for price negotiation to determine fair value for equity distribution. However, organizations have to be careful about how to manage the benefactors of existing endowments, and sensitive to the concerns of students, faculty, and alumni of the merging organizations.

In addition to mergers and acquisitions, institutions should consider collaborative arrangements for academic support. It is not necessary for an institution to provide all courses required for a degree offering. It would be more cost effective if certain courses, with low enrollments, were provided by another institution on a purchased or course exchange basis. This subject is discussed in more depth in Chapter 12. In any event, it is clear that beneficial long-range planning will accelerate in the American higher education industry.

FOR FURTHER READING

Buhler-Miko, Marina. *A Trustee's Guide to Strategic Planning*. Washington, DC: Higher Education Planning Institute, 1985.

Cope, Robert G. *Opportunity from Strength: Strategic Planning Clarified with Case Examples*. ASHE-ERIC Higher Education Report no. 8. Washington, DC: Association for the Study of Higher Education, 1987.

Keller, George. *Academic Strategy*. Baltimore, MD: Johns Hopkins University Press, 1983.

CHAPTER 5

•••••••••

The Operating Budget

C hief financial officers often have great difficulty installing professional budget systems with all the checks and balances and controls necessary to satisfy the purpose of budgets. Most financial organizations within higher education are still structured so that the budget officer is on an equal organizational level with the controller. In turn, both report to the position normally designated CFO (chief financial officer). Such a structure is ineffective because it relegates the CFO to the position of controller and subordinates the controller to the position of accounting manager. If the controller does not have responsibility for budgets, then the individual is not truly a controller and is more of a comptroller or plant accountant.

To be a controller, the individual occupying that position must be fully responsible not only for actual accounting information but for all budgetary aspects, including enrollment commitments, financial aid discounting commitments, personnel organizations, operating expenses, debt service, and other expenditures that constitute the entire operating statement of the organization. The very title of controller recognizes that this is the individual responsible for maintaining all financial systems, reporting management's commitments regarding revenues and expenditures, and interpreting financial results for the year. Separating the budget officer and the controller is an unfortunate "divide and conquer" aproach to budgeting in higher education.

The fact that higher education is identified as a not-for-profit organization means that the attitude of all concerned is that the operation should roughly break even each year. This budgetary attitude is also consistent with that in government, where the purpose of a budget is to achieve spending in total for all individual accounts so that the pluses equal the minuses and the monies are spent in their entirety; the result is a break-even situation, hence the "spend it or lose it" mind-set. Figure 5.1 shows an example of the traditional organization for the financial function in higher education and the recommended structure.

This chapter bridges two other chapters that constitute the strategic overview for financial planning and control within an organization. Chapter 4 outlined strategic long-term planning; Chapter 6 outlines costing and pricing. Financial planning and control are very much interrelated. The development of a long-term plan requires that costing and pricing be in place in order to work out the strategy and timing of an organization's ambitions while remaining financially viable. As mentioned in the previous chapter, a strategic long-term plan should be approved by management and reviewed by the board of trustees annually prior to initiating preparation of operating budgets for the following year. In effect, the specific plans that have gone into the first of the five years in the planning exercise constitute the guidelines to be used in developing the one-year operating budget. When the operating budget is completed and approved, it should be the detailed commitment of the truncated first year of the five-year strategic plan. The operating budget, in effect, is an indexing control system for achieving strategic plans on a year-to-year basis. The controller, supported by the budget manager, is responsible for pulling together the following major categories of revenue and expenditures for assembling an operating budget for the institution:

Revenue Sources	Expenditures
Tuition and fees	Instruction
Sponsored research	Administrative departments
Endowment support	Capital equipment
Gifts and grants	Debt service
Investment income	Reserve requirements
Auxiliary enterprises	Auxiliary enterprises
	Contingency

REVENUE SOURCES

The first step in preparing a budget is to determine what the expected revenues will be for the year. For higher education institutions, the primary source of revenue will be tuition and fees, and will be developed around marketing strategy based on competitive factors that influence price for tuition, quality and volume of student enrollments, and the financial aid discounting and marketing expenditures necessary to achieve the planned enrollment levels.

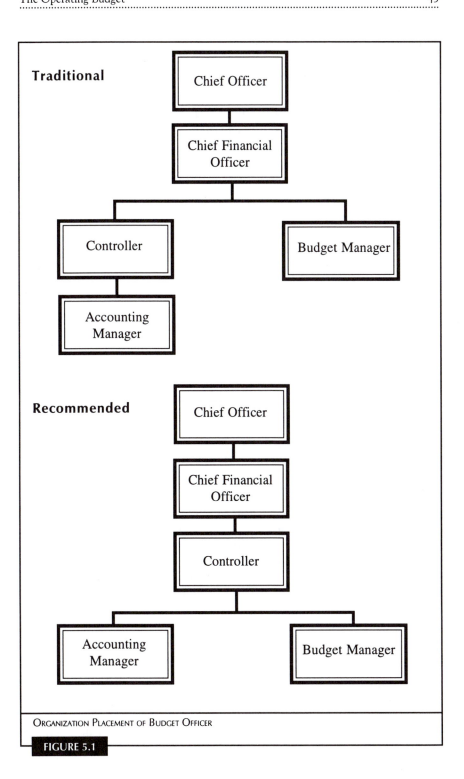

ORGANIZATION PLACEMENT OF BUDGET OFFICER

FIGURE 5.1

In addition to primary revenues from instruction and research, many organizations support their current operations with a subsidy from unrestricted endowments. The subsidy is usually based on a spending rate that has been agreed upon by the board of trustees and determined by earnings on the quasi-endowments. In addition, there may be other forms of support from third-party endowments such as professorships and facility maintenance. Gifts and grants are an ongoing, unrestricted form of revenue that is usually based on some historical growth track with most of the funds being derived through annual gifts from alumni of the institution.

Short-term investment income is the earnings realized on working capital of the institution. Higher education is fortunate that most of its income (tuition and fees) is received in two large amounts during the year. This provides an opportunity to invest these monies in short-term notes that provide an income to current operations until the funds are required.

The last category of revenue is auxiliary enterprises. In order to keep the presentation of budgeting to a simple conceptual approach, examples of an institution that has teaching hospitals, major athletic programs, and other sources of revenues are not included. Auxiliary enterprises, therefore, in this example are primarily room and board and other revenues derived from the usage of the facilities of the institution. In determining the room and board, it is necessary first to anticipate the enrollments, the number of students who will opt for residency, and those who will be on a food plan. Marketing strategy is useful here in comparing residence and food prices to other sources of local competition. When the revenue items outlined above are analyzed and priced, it will be possible to determine if total revenues from all sources approximate those outlined in the strategic plan and approximate the categories as determined at the time the plan was developed.

An institution with an up-to-date strategic plan should furnish it to all department heads and chairs as well as deans. The management of those institutions that do not have a strategic plan should prepare assumptions that will be used to support preparation of the operating budget. In addition to enrollment figures, the assumptions should include economic factors, anticipated problems, planned changes to the organization or facilities, and any other information necessary for department heads to have a basic understanding of what is expected of their organization.

EXPENDITURES

The first item under expenditures is the classroom instruction budgets. Enrollment information by school and by college will allow department chairs, deans, and the provost to prepare anticipated sections, class sizes, and faculty loading. As will be seen in Chapter 6, instruction budgeting will be crucial during the continued downsizing of higher education during the 1990s in order to avoid seat costs in the classroom increasing at an exponential rate. (The specific problems associated with seat costs during a downsizing situation are detailed in Chapter 12.)

Higher education is a labor-intensive business with more than half of all expenditures representing salary and fringe benefits. If an institution can control its organization structure and the personnel in those organization charts, it can contain most of the expenditures for higher education. Most expenditures other than personnel expenditures directly support personnel; if the personnel figures are kept to a minimum, the other accounts, including facility needs, will also be kept to a minimum. For this reason, the primary feature in the operating budget for each department is an organization chart. In an organization with tight controls on personnel, the organization chart will consist of a box for each existing position in the organization with a slot number for that position, a title, a reporting relationship, a salary administration pay grade, and current salary of the incumbent. The key to controlling personnel is maintaining close coordination between the budget manager, the payroll department, and the salary administrator in the human resource department. With such coordination, nobody can be hired, fired, promoted, etc., unless he or she is contained in the slot system in the human resource department and the corresponding position on the organization chart within the budget department.

In preparing budgets, department heads should first review their organization and make any anticipated changes to the charts such as addition or deletion of personnel, promotions, and organization structure changes.

Reviewing the organization budget at least once a year at budget time also provides the opportunity for department heads to present proposed changes in operations or cost reductions that might increase efficiency. These proposals should be an integral part of the budget exercise, but should also stand alone in order that management can pass judgment on the merits of proposed organization structure changes. Certainly a proposed change should include the rationale for the change, benefits to be derived, pros and cons of the change, and a financial analysis to support the proposal.

Preparation of the administrative department budgets also includes completion of the nonpersonnel expenditure accounts to support the organization chart as proposed. Among the nonpersonnel accounts are travel and entertainment, supplies, materials, reproduction, advertising, facility alterations, professional services, leases, and consultants.

The last major category before moving to institutional considerations is capital equipment. Capital equipment is a major budget item in higher education because of the number of personnel to be supported with equipment, buildings to house a people-intensive business, support services for the buildings, and, in recent years, the extraordinary proliferation of computers and other electronic data equipment. Budget requests for equipment/facilities should be supported with rationales and analyses that justify need whether the requests be for additional capital items or replacement of existing equipment/ facilities.

Institutional requirements for debt service, reserve requirements, and contingencies should be developed by the controller in conjunction with the officers. Debt service includes the mortgages on the physical plant. Mortgages and the resultant debt service are determined by projecting construction costs for facilities and deducting any third-party giving or excess institution funds available to determine the amount that must be mortgaged. Debt service in the budget year represents outstanding mortgage bonds, less any that might mature, plus debt service on mortgage bonds to be added.

Reserves are monies set aside for expected future expenditures. Examples would be reserve monies set aside for restoration and replacement of facilities, major computer changes, and administrative/academic system conversion programs.

Auxiliary enterprises make up the "business" side of higher education if generating revenues in excess of expenditures is determined to be appropriate. Whereas research is frequently a losing proposition and instruction less than a break-even proposition, higher education survives in great part because of the business side of operations, which is primarily room and board. The means of support for a resident institution with room and board margins are reviewed in depth in Chapter 8.

Resident students will provide financial salvation for many institutions in the next decade if declining enrollment figures do not exceed the room and board rate increases because fixed costs for resident building debt service will be stable and in many institutions decline as mortgages are paid down. Ironically, as tuition revenues/margins shrink with the demographic decline and revenues/margins remain stable for room and board within auxiliary enterprises, higher education will become less tuition dependent. Becoming less tuition dependent has been a goal of many institutions but hardly at the risk of losing the institution.

Operating budgets should contain certain contingencies. Many astute department heads will overstate certain expenditures to provide a cushion or a contingency at their level. However, formal contingencies should be established at the officer or trustee level. Operating budgets are normally prepared about 18 months before the last dollar is collected or spent, and it is difficult, if not impossible, to anticipate every change that might occur during that 18-month period. For this reason, to avoid deficits, it is a good idea to establish contingencies, which if they are not used can be passed through as excess margin for that year and either transferred to quasi-endowments or set up as an additional reserve input.[1]

Contingencies serve three purposes. First, if the monies are not required during the year, they can be transferred into the quasi-endowments along with any other excesses that may be realized during the year; or, they can be allowed to accumulate in the current fund balance. Second, they can be used for unexpected major expenditures or initiation of new programs. Third, they can serve as a buffer if there is a revenue shortfall, particularly in the enrollment area.

Institutions handle excesses in different ways. Some retain the entire excess in current operations, others transfer all or part to quasi-endowments, while some separate and transfer amounts to other funds to establish desired balances. I favor sweeping all excesses at the end of the year into the quasi-endowments if not required elsewhere and maintaining a zero balance in the current fund. This approach serves multiple purposes: (1) it gives the appearance of a break-even operation and, therefore, fulfills the government's direction to operate a not-for-profit business; (2) it strengthens the balance sheet because it consolidates reserves and fund balances in the quasi-endowments facilitating calculations of average endowment per student; and (3) it avoids the need to run a deficit in the current fund to use monies contained in the fund balance.

ASSEMBLING A BUDGET

Budgets should be a bottom-up exercise. The only way to hold individuals responsible for spending is to allow them to prepare the budget for their area, defend that budget, and, once approved, be held responsible for the budget. This approach provides a grassroots buildup of every function within the organization. Also, do not attempt to hold department heads responsible for expenditures that they can't control, such as allocated expenditures. (Allocations and the purpose they serve regarding a project/program cost system will be reviewed in Chapter 6.)

For appropriate budgeting, it is a good idea to set up an encumbrance system through the purchasing and accounts payable departments. An encumbrance system provides an early warning for accounts that reflect cost-to-date and purchase commitments that might throw them into excess of the total budget for the year. Figure 5.2 demonstrates an encumbrance system.

In the example in Figure 5.2, Item 2 is in trouble at the time of the requested encumbrances of $4,000 because requisition of all encumbered material will place the item in overrun against the total year budget.

---

[1]Robert N. Anthony and Regina E. Herzlinger, eds., *Management Control in Nonprofit Organizations* (Homewood, IL: Richard D. Irwin, Inc., 1975), 286.

Item	Month			Year to Date			Encumber	Expected for Year	Budget for Year	Variance
	Budget	Actual	Variance	Budget	Actual	Variance				
1	$ 100	$ 75	$ 25	$ 400	$ 375	$ 25				
2	500	550	(50)	3,000	2,000	1,000	$4,000	$6,000	$5,000	$(1,000)
3	700	800	(100)	1,500	1,000	500	400	1,400	2,000	600
Total	$1,300	$1,425	$(125)	$4,900	$3,375	$1,525				

ENCUMBRANCE SYSTEM: AN UNFAVORABLE EXAMPLE

FIGURE 5.2

Invariably, the first summary of requested departmental budgets will exceed that which the division vice president had anticipated for the year or is willing to accept from his or her department heads and defend to the budget committee. All department heads and deans should have an opportunity to review their proposals with their respective vice presidents. Upon acceptance, the vice presidents will then be responsible for defending the division budget to the budget committee, consisting of vice presidents along with the controller and the budget manager.

The next step in assembling a budget for the institution is for the controller, supported by the budget manager, to summarize the entire institution, including revenues, expenditures, transfers, and institutional items anticipated for the year. The summary should be presented to the budget committee for review. Again, a first summary of expenditures and transfers will invariably exceed that which is available in revenues. At the minimum, review at this level should consist of the following:

- A review of each division's organization chart with particular attention paid to requested new positions and the rationale for changes in structure. New position requests are difficult to evaluate because, at this point in the request for position needs, the budget office and the salary administrator have not had an opportunity to review thoroughly the position to determine need. The most difficult part of the assessment is determining whether a new position is truly a full-time demand. If the position can not generate a productive 2,000 hours of labor a year, it is not really required and the organization should be restructured to absorb what is anticipated to be additional workload.
- Capital equipment requests are difficult to assess. Requests for equipment that improves the environment, particularly in terms of safety, should be seriously considered. Frequently, requests for replacement of existing equipment fall under the category of analysis regarding financial justification, obsolescence, or safety. For those items that

are justified on a financial basis, the payoff period should be shortened if there are cash flow problems. (Payoff period is calculated by dividing the investment by annual savings. A $10,000 investment saving $2,500 a year is equivalent to earnings of approximately 20 percent on the investment. The payout is four years, and after adjustment of 25 percent for compound value, the earnings are about 20 percent if the investment could earn 10 percent per year.)

- Marketing is not only a difficult area to assess but historically in higher education has been decentralized and parochial. If managers are doing their job, they are not only watching individual marketing efforts on the campus, but are arranging for them to be coordinated centrally. In a downsizing mode, institutions have to take a hard look at which programs should be continued and which ones should be downsized or discontinued to make facility capacity available for another school or program able to generate a larger margin. Marketing, as a function, should include admissions, public relations, media, publications, and other internal and external communication functions.

- The rapid buildup of internally provided financial aid, by means of tuition discounting, will break many institutions in the 1990s. It is impossible for institutions to make up the difference in the loss of subsidy from state and federal governments while trying to address a median family income that is shrinking relative to the cost of higher education. Those institutions that control their costs and market price will have the advantage of being able to exist with a lower percentage of financial aid discount. If an institution can convince the public that it is providing quality education equal to or greater than competitive institutions at a lower price, the public will beat a path to its door.

- The physical plant has been a problem for the past 20 years. It was and remains a major area of expenditures that can be delayed to buy time until perceived "happy days" return again. Management will have to bite the bullet and ensure appropriate spending on the physical plant to avoid further deterioration of facilities in the face of a mounting backlog of deferred maintenance.

- Finally, the toughest major area of budgetary control will be holding down faculty costs per seat in the classroom. I will not dwell on the subject because Chapter 12 has been devoted to the subject of academics and faculty. It was written to identify the many reasons for escalating instruction cost, which became a problem during years of expansion and will become acute in a downsizing mode.

The vice presidents, controller, and the budget manager should review each division's organization, new programs, changes in personnel spending trends, and capital requests to ensure that all members of the committee are comfortable with the budgets as presented and defended. The end goal of the budget committee should be to bring the budget as close to balance between revenue flow and spending as possible.

The president should next be presented with the operating budget as prepared by the vice presidents and the controller. The budget should include all major data and supporting schedules to disclose trends and problems. Once the president has reviewed the package in its entirety with the financial officer, it is time to schedule meetings with the individual vice presidents to defend their budgets.

With full knowledge of the budget as assembled, the president now assumes the position of leadership and earns his or her keep. It is the president who must lead the final charge on what will be assembled as an operating budget for presentation to the board of trustees. Tough decisions have to be made regarding what remains in the budget, what gets delayed, and what gets removed completely in order to balance the budget and maintain consistency with the long-term strategic plan it supports and the ultimate vision of the chief officer. The chief officer must personally accept, endorse, and present the budget.

The budget is now complete and ready for presentation to the board. The chief officer owns it and the vice presidents accept and will support the budget as approved by the chief officer.

ADMINISTRATING THE BUDGET

A chapter on operating budgets written by a business officer would not be complete without a listing of Robert's Rules (i.e., the author's rules). The budget is an ongoing process that acts as a control program for ensuring that management personnel at all levels are held accountable for achieving the goals to which they committed at the time they collectively prepared a budget for the institution. Robert's Rules for sound budgetary control are as follows:

- Department heads should be held accountable for their budget performance on a monthly basis by their respective vice president.
- Vice presidents should be held responsible by the chief officer on a quarterly basis to provide an explanation for variances and plans to bring the budget back in line if there are variances developing.
- Funds should not be transferred between accounts during the year unless there is a functional or organizational change that precipitates a legitimate transfer. Illegitimate transfers between accounts only serve to (1) cover up poor budgeting; (2) avoid variances; (3) make the accounts look good; (4) destroy historical relationships and trends within the accounts; and (5) accommodate the intent of many to fully

use and spend all funds available rather than underspend and make funds available for other programs or generate excesses for the future development of the institution. Transfers also defeat the purpose of variance analysis to determine the reasons why thinking and circumstances regarding spending changed from the original intent.

- Personnel accounts, which include salary and wages of full-time and part-time personnel, overtime, as well as agency help, should stand apart from the nonpersonnel budget accounts. Underspending in the nonpersonnel accounts is not a rationale for hiring additional help.
- An item listed in the budget is not an automatic authorization to spend. Thousands of decisions on thousands of items are brought together quickly at the time the annual budget is prepared. For this reason, their "acceptance" in the budget does not constitute approval to spend at a later date. When it is time to spend on personnel, the job description should first be completed, classified, and the position again justified. In the case of nonpersonnel items, requisitions should be written for appropriate approval at the time the money is spent. Circumstances change with time and every day is a new day with changing priorities.
- The operating budget should be revisited and reforecasted two or three times a year to see if year-end results will still match those of the original budget. Problems are better addressed if identified early. Conversely, good news, such as excess revenues, should be disclosed as soon as possible in case there are pressing needs or other priorities that might be established with this knowledge.
- If a forecast discloses that there is a major financial problem or a significant enrollment shortfall, the budget for the year should be redone in detail. However, well-thought-out budgets, with contingency positions, seldom require a rebudget exercise.
- Accounts within the budget should be carefully defined so that everybody in the institution charges similar expenses to the same account. Without a clear definition, it would be impossible to collect institutionwide summary data and prepare trend analyses or compare common budgets. In fact, in certain accounts, such as travel, there should be subaccounts to collect data by type of travel such as conferences, presentation of papers, fund raising, and admissions/ marketing. This level of delineation is crucial for the development of a meaningful cost system.
- Every attempt should be made to achieve quality performance while underspending the budget.

The annual budget exercise, which is a process that addresses operational activities in the current fund, is also an opportunity to manage the balance sheet. In reviewing the various funds of an institution, bankers and bonds people are sensitive to an institution's level of endowment, particularly the endowment per full-time equivalent student, and unrestricted funds that are available to the institution to offset long-term debt. For these two reasons, it is important that all reserves and fund balances, to whatever extent possible, be consolidated within the endowment funds under quasi-endowment. Quasi-endowment includes retained earnings, unrestricted gifts, and the earnings on the fund. Restricted endowments are wonderful. However, unrestricted endowments or quasi-endowments are the retained earnings that will save many institutions during the 1990s.

Bankers know that quasi-endowments provide discretionary money; there isn't any better ratio an institution can maintain than to have enough quasi-endowment to pay off all long-term debt. In addition, collection of discretionary funds within the quasi-endowment under the Endowments and Similar Funds budget heading allows a rating agency to divide the fund balance by full-time equivalent students and arrive at an average endowment figure per student.

Finally, as higher education fine-tunes its budget processes and prepares to batten down the hatches for the financial difficulties to come, it would be a good idea to have an outside consulting group review the organization structure and all positions in the organization. It is impossible for people within an organization to be totally objective about their approach to organization and personnel requirements, particularly during downsizing. Management frequently is reluctant to bring in a third-party consultant because doing so can be construed as an admission that management cannot conduct an objective review. It may also disturb the functions for which managers are responsible and force change; disclose something that has been hidden; result in downsizing, consolidation, or elimination of an organization that was carefully built over the years; be too difficult and time consuming; or be an embarrassment and make individuals look bad. Although a comprehensive review by a consulting firm is expensive, in the long run it will pay handsome rewards. In fact, it could be one of the best investments the institution has ever made.

FINAL ADVICE

Reconstitute your budget process before attempting to address development of a cost system. Get a cost system integrated with the budget process up and running as soon as possible to provide support for long-term strategic planning (see Chapter 6).

Prepare a budget/cost operating manual with schedules and spreadsheets. This will ensure an understanding of the processes and a common approach to data preparation and collection.

FOR FURTHER READING

Anthony, Robert N., and Herzlinger, Regina E., eds. *Management Control in Nonprofit Organizations.* Homewood, IL: Richard D. Irwin, Inc., 1975.

Firstenberg, Paul B. *Managing for Profit in the Nonprofit World.* New York: The Foundation Center, 1986.

Gambino, Anthony J. *Planning and Control in Higher Education.* New York: National Association of Accountants, 1979.

CHAPTER 6

Costing and Pricing

Many institutions of higher education are still struggling with the basics of installing a bottom-up approach to developing annual budgets for controlling expenditures by operating department. For those institutions with no sound budgeting procedures and practices in place, this chapter will prove difficult because it focuses on costing and pricing—a giant step beyond departmental operating budgets. Few colleges have cost systems in place; by the year 2000 the surviving institutions will have such systems.

In the previous chapters on strategic long-term planning and operating budgets, the purpose and foundation for development of a costing system were established. The difference between budgeting and costing, particularly in higher education, can be viewed as a matrix. Budget items are under the control of an operating department manager and expenditures represent one side of a summary matrix, while the summary information running down the matrix is a costing, a collection of the same figures in a different order by project or program. A matrix for this relationship is shown in Figure 6.1, which suggests only the basic structure of a costing system. A comprehensive system should provide detail by college, school, academic discipline, institute, research project, type of residential accommodation, etc. The system should also provide cost detail on programs that do not generate income. Note that Figure 6.1 does not include the budget/cost for the institutional advancement division. Fund-raising activities are unique to the not-for-profit business sector. Funds raised are the third form of asset formulation singularly equivalent to sale of stock but without ownership. (The other two forms of asset accumulation, equity [accumulated earnings] and debt, are common to both for-profit

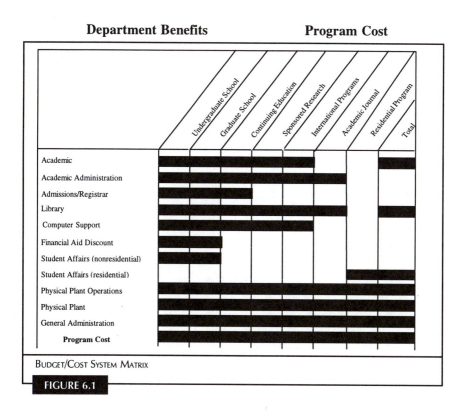

Department Benefits   **Program Cost**

BUDGET/COST SYSTEM MATRIX

FIGURE 6.1

and not-for-profit businesses.) Performance measurement of fund-raising activities of the institutional advancement division is reviewed in Chapter 9.

THE PURPOSE OF A COST SYSTEM

The purpose of developing a cost system for an institution of higher education
is to determine what programs cost relative to the revenue they are capable of
generating. Some programs generate excesses that can be used elsewhere in
the organization, others lose money, and some barely break even. Without
proper analysis by program, it is impossible for management to know why
overall performance for the institution is not what they would expect it to be.
Traditionally, there is a cost separation between academics and auxiliary
enterprises, although even these segregated costs often can be misleading.
Proper cost by program not only separates the winners from the losers but
provides trends when compared to previous years to observe if a program's
performance, from a financial point of view, is getting better or worse. For
costing to be meaningful, it must compare cost to the revenues associated with

the project being analyzed. The cost system will provide comparative results by project in the same manner that the budget system provides comparison by department. For a whole array of reasons, it is essential that the computer module for the cost system be integrated with the module for the budget system. Handling the same numbers twice in separate systems would be inefficient.

Costing will gain in importance during the remainder of the 1990s as higher education is forced to move away from its practice of establishing prices on a cost plus basis. Tuition pricing will become competitive and higher education will be forced to use cost analysis and cost control as a means of living with prices that are no longer elastic. Costing will provide the opportunity to determine which programs generate sufficient margin to warrant their continuation or to accept, in certain cases, their loss contribution because of their need and impact on overall operations.

Instituting cost systems in higher education will be particularly troublesome because so many costs incurred within operating department budgets indirectly support many projects/programs. For this reason, there is the continuous problem of appropriately segregating costs as they best apply to a given activity. Without proper segregation, cost versus revenue reports generated could be terribly misleading and force management to make improper decisions. Costs must be distributed on the basis of what shared cost is appropriate support to a given program. Well-conceived allocation formulas and bases must be developed to provide appropriate and equitable distribution of certain operating expenses to the various projects and programs the department supports.

The dearth of cost analysis in higher education can be appreciated if we recognize what the environment has been to date. As mentioned previously, the business and its revenues have been historically developed on the basis of revenue need. This forced a cost-plus approach for establishing price, which determined revenue flow for an institution of higher education. With few major interruptions over the last 350 years, there has been sustained enrollment growth that provided a sustained revenue flow comfortably paying for absorption of new cost (and weak management). In addition, such not-for-profits appeared to be cost effective because the institutions were not expected to earn a profit, only survive. With this mind-set, management has not been held responsible for achieving a bottom line result and, therefore, has not been conscientious about costs in general, let alone their identification by the many programs within an institution. The combination of growth and no expectation for financial performance, along with the fact that there has been no real pressure on employees because of protection from tenure and no concern about layoffs among administrators, set the stage for problems in the 1990s.

This mind-set fastened the image of academia as an easygoing way of life with quiet summers. These circumstances add up to one overriding concern: Does the environment engender a positive work ethic and productivity?

Without a work ethic and with a cavalier attitude concerning costs, you have a business that is postured for problems in a business downturn. Exacerbating this condition was a willingness by higher education to help students financially by allowing a proliferation of unproductive jobs for them to perform in lieu of partial tuition payment. As young developing professionals, the students have been able to provide workload relief for faculty, administrators, and the secretaries supporting the professionals. In practice, you have a situation similar to the old military establishment where an orderly was assigned to each officer to serve personal needs—a throwback to a quiet, bygone era.

A PRIMER ON COSTING

Although this chapter was not written to be a "how to" document on accounting, it is necessary that costing be explained so that the reader can appreciate the detail and purpose of cost programs. The difference between budgeting and costing has already been outlined in the spending matrix. The following terminology is necessary for a basic understanding of costing:

Fixed and Variable Costs

Fixed costs, for the most part, are indifferent to changes in business volume. However, all fixed costs can or should become variable if business volume declines appreciably. Examples of fixed costs are facilities, officers, debt service, and long-term leases.

Variable costs have a direct relationship with business volume, which in higher education is primarily the level of enrollment. Variable costs include part-time faculty, staff, fringe benefits, travel, and supplies. Variable costs can be added or deleted, depending on changes in the revenue base supported.

Direct and Indirect Costs

Direct costs are incurred in direct support of a program, project, department, or a section.

Indirect costs are incurred in direct support of a collection of common endeavors. Examples would be secretarial support, travel, material and supplies, and telephones in support of a group of faculty members. The faculty members are a direct cost for instruction; thus their departmental support costs are distributed as a percentage of faculty direct labor cost (or by proportion of faculty count).

All direct and indirect costs can be further segregated into fixed and variable categories.

Controllable Costs

All costs are controllable, but what is important is at what level of the organization they are controllable and who is assigned responsibility for a specific cost category. In any cost system, it is extremely important that an individual project or program manager be held responsible for costs that are fully under his or her control.

Costs that are allocated to a program should be carefully defined against a basis that provides equitable absorption of common costs. Although a program manager can not directly control assigned or allocated cost, he or she can influence their absorption by controlling the basis on which certain costs are assigned, such as square footage of space utilized.

Allocated Costs

These are costs that can not be specifically identified with an operation, for example, general and administrative expenses for officers or legal and audit expenditures. Costs of these types should be collected in budget cost centers and allocated to specific operations, usually on a relative program cost basis.

For example, if total program costs for an institution are $5,700,000 and total general and administrative costs are $750,000, each project/program will be allocated 13.16 percent against its program cost ($750,000 divided by $5,700,000). Therefore, if the graduate school has an operating cost of $2,585,000, it will be allocated $340,186 for general and administrative expenses ($2,585,000 x 13.16 percent = $340,186).

Incremental Costs and Revenues

This cost/revenue consideration is a bugaboo in any business and is particularly troublesome in higher education because of the general lack of cost experience and understanding. The addition of volume in any business provides for a reduction in per unit cost because fixed costs are absorbed on a larger base, reducing unit/student cost. For those who are not familiar with accounting, it leads to the belief that all units after the first unit do not create additional fixed cost and, therefore, subsequent units should not absorb any of the fixed cost. If this were true, then incremental, out-of-pocket, and variable cost would all be identical. This is cost absorption misrepresentation.

Incremental costs are like using debt as leverage in the stock market. When enrollments are rising, the shrinking fixed cost per unit provides for greater margins. Conversely, when volume is going down, the fixed costs are spread over a smaller base and the margin per unit shrinks dramatically. The only time incremental costs should be considered is if one wants to adjust price to affect volume and the resultant impact on margin. This is a legitimate and effective use of incremental costing.

An example in higher education would be incremental revenue that could be realized if empty seats in a classroom were filled. This could be achieved by offering certain students a significantly discounted tuition to register in a class with empty seats after all other students have registered. This same concept could also be applied to empty beds in the resident buildings. The concept of using incremental costing as it relates to tuition discounting is reviewed in Chapter 14.

If curriculum development is the engineering of higher education, then instruction is the manufacturing component of the business. To establish a cost system for programs, schools, and colleges, faculty costs must be identified by discipline and by the various schools in order to relate those direct costs for instruction to the revenue generated by the students in their respective teaching sections.

Developing intricate cost systems today is much easier that it was 40 years ago before the advent of the computer for gathering and assigning business data. With an appropriate software module, the following data should be gathered for proper cost analysis regarding instruction. All data gathered should start at a basic level, which is by individual faculty member. The database should include base salary, less portion bought out for research; number of sections taught; and number of students in each section. The next step is to develop an overhead rate to be applied to the professors, which accounts for the time they spend on administrative matters for the common good of the institution. The overhead rate can be developed by discipline or as an overall rate for the entire faculty body within a given school or college. Whichever method is chosen, the items to be included in the overhead are stipends paid for scholarly activities beyond base salaries, such as stipends paid for work performed by a professor during the summer months; assigned time to act as a department chair; responsibility for an institute or a magazine; internal scholarly activity; or sabbaticals.

AN EXAMPLE OF COSTING

With the above understanding of how to cost faculty, Figure 6.2 presents a simulation of costing for a given discipline within a school or college.

	Undergraduate	Graduate	Total
Gross Tuition Revenue	$4,500,000	$3,000,000	$7,500,000
Less: Financial Aid	900,000	300,000	1,200,000
Net Tuition Revenue	$3,600,000	$2,700,000	$6,300,000
Direct Cost			
Instruction	$2,050,000	$1,700,000	$3,750,000
Indirect Cost			
Instruction Overhead	525,000	475,000	1,000,000
Facility Cost	100,000	150,000	250,000
Subtotal	$2,675,000	$2,325,000	$5,000,000
Number of Seats Utilized	3,450 63%*	2,000 37%*	5,450
Net Revenue Per Seat	$1,045	$1,350	$1,155
Direct/Indirect Cost Per Seat	775	1,165	915
Instruction Margin Per Seat	$ 270	$ 185	$ 240
Margins % Net Revenue (FTE)	26%	14%	21%
Allocated Costs			
Admission/Registration/Aid			$200,000
Library			400,000
Computer Support			100,000
Subtotal	$440,000 63%	$260,000 37%	$700,000
Total Program Cost	$3,115,000 55%*	$2,585,000 45%*	$5,700,000
General Administration	410,000 55%	$340,000 45%	$750,000
Total Operating Cost	$3,525,000	$2,925,000	$6,450,000
Operating Margin (Loss)	$75,000	$(225,000)	$(150,000)

*Calculation for proportional distribution of allocated costs.

GENERAL EDUCATIONAL COSTING EXAMPLE

FIGURE 6.2

The hypothetical costing example is a conceptual summary of primary information required for developing function and operating margins for an institutional activity. In this example, we pick up direct cost, which is the instruction salaries and benefits of the faculty; direct overhead; and facility cost.

The section outlined in the box develops the necessary indices to evaluate margin at the instruction level by "seat." Although higher education has developed FTE (full-time equivalent) student indices, an appropriate cost system on a computer would be much better served by the "common revenue/cost factor" of student loading by classroom seat (hospitals have already recognized a similar need using "bed" revenue/cost). The revenue/cost system can be developed using existing faculty loading, classroom assignment, and student registration systems.

In this hypothetical example, the undergraduate school is providing a 26 percent margin versus a 14 percent margin for the graduate school. If a school does not generate a margin at the instruction level, significant losses will be incurred at the institution level after all expenses are absorbed.

Facility costs are developed in a separate budget for all operating costs associated with supporting the physical plant. Usually these costs are collected in total and then distributed to various operations according to the square footage space used. In this example, classroom and office space for the faculty and their support personnel is accounted for by direct utilization. It should be noted that other cost centers, like admissions/registrar or the library, already contain their own facility costs. The development of facility space costs is reviewed in Chapter 13.

Admissions, registrar, and financial aid departments were allocated on the basis of seats used along with the library and computer support. General administrative expenses were distributed on the basis of total program cost. The institution shows a loss at the operating level of $150,000 with the undergraduate program showing a margin of $75,000 and the graduate school a loss of $225,000. Many institutions will find upon proper cost evaluation that certain academic programs lose money.

A good question to ask at this point is the following: If most institutions lose money at the operating level, then why do most of them over time either break even or generate slight excesses from general operations? The answer is straightforward. Ancillary enterprises, which include room and board and other business ventures along with gifts, investment income, and funds received in the form of endowments and grants, are the monies that enable the typical institution to absorb losses incurred from the primary business of education.

OTHER CATEGORIES OF COSTING

Now that a general costing approach has been established that can be used by discipline or by school, it is appropriate to list the many other areas that constitute pockets of business with their own revenue base. Costs can be compared to other activities of the institution to track performance and trends for those individual programs.

Instruction

- By discipline
- By school/college
- By research in total and by major projects
- By institute
- By event
- By journal, publication, etc.
- By program

Auxiliary Enterprises

- By resident activity in total as well as by type of accommodation
- By food program in total as well as by individual offerings
- By support function
- By varsity athletic program
- By services

Conferencing
(rental of facilities to outside organizations)

- By individual conferencing event
- By residential program in the summer and nonresidential programs throughout the year
- By types of event, such as precollegiate, athletic camp, industry conferences, etc.
- By total conferencing summary

BENEFITS OF A SOUND COSTING SYSTEM

A sound costing system for margin evaluation and development of prices will provide visibility on which programs are carrying their weight. It is recognized that some programs are necessary as building blocks for other functions within the institution and that some serve as public relations activities for recruiting students or projecting institution image in the marketplace. Without a cost system, management cannot know how programs are doing, except on a consolidated basis from annual operating results. Without costing, it is impossible to know which operations are slipping off from their expected performance, what they are contributing to the whole, and what changes should be made in structure or mission to consolidate or reduce spending. It is also impossible to provide dependable revenue, cost, and margin simulation support for long-term strategic planning.

A sound costing system is essential for proper management and survival. The following are some advantages to an institution that installs a cost system:

- The academic division will be able to manage financial performance by disciplines, schools (day, evening, and summer sessions), as well as between colleges at the university level.
- The academic division will be able to evaluate strategic business alliance opportunities with other institutions.
- Management will be able to judge the financial significance of a merger with another institution, particularly if the other institution also has a cost system in place.
- Management will be able to address problem programs and make appropriate decisions regarding pricing and organization changes if required.
- Management will have the data to make informed organization or management personnel changes.
- Management will become aware of problems created by fixed costs during the downsizing of higher education in the 1990s and will be motivated to address solutions.
- Management will be able to proceed with the next level of business development—strategic planning. A sound costing system will provide the institutional research personnel the ability to study past cost factors and apply parametric pricing formulas to business planning projections.
- A revenue/cost simulation model can be built from the cost system for support of long-term strategic planning.
- The board of trustees will be able to establish performance objectives for the president and vice presidents.

The costing example used in this chapter did not address the incremental cost situation facing evening schools. Most facility and general administrative costs would be allocated to the full-time day undergraduate and graduate schools because these costs exist for their purpose. Evening schools can therefore contribute a positive cash flow on a smaller margin per seat percentage. This is possible because there is little incremental cost added to make secondary use of campus facilities and services.

In conclusion, it is difficult for management to ask the right questions if they don't have cost detail and visibility concerning ongoing events within their institution. A sound costing system integrated with the operating budget and the long-term strategic planning programs will become an essential management tool in higher education.

FOR FURTHER READING

Bulloch, James; Keller, Donald E.; and Vlasho, Louis, eds. *Accountants' Cost Handbook: A Guide for Management Accounting*. 3d ed. New York: John Wiley and Sons, 1983.

Turk, Frederick J. "Activity Based Costing." *National Symposium on Strategic Higher Education Finance & Management Issues: Proceedings*. Washington, DC: National Association of College and University Business Officers, 1991.

U.S. Department of Education. *Tough Choices: A Guide to Administrative Cost Management in Colleges and Universities*. Washington, DC: Department of Education, 1991.

CHAPTER 7

Marketing the Institution

Institutions are established to accomplish a particular mission or need, and, like any business, require many years to establish a product and develop a niche in the marketplace. The market for any product changes with time and society's needs, and for this reason an institution must continually assess the marketplace and redefine mission and curriculum. This chapter on marketing closely follows the chapter on strategic long-term planning because development of a marketing program should be predicated on the strategic plans of the institution.

Marketing higher education has become an absolute necessity in recent years because of a decline in customer base. Higher education in the United States was established in 1636 by the king's land grant for Harvard College. The industry has been fortunate that, with the exception of temporary wartime periods and an economic depression, there was almost 350 years of uninterrupted growth in population, which provided an expanding market for institutions of higher education. Coupled with uninterrupted growth in population was society's developing need for citizens with education beyond high school to manage the expanding economy and technology of the country. In 1979, all this changed when changing demographics resulted in a reduced number of 18-year-olds available to pursue higher education. Institutions wishing to maintain enrollment, protect revenue flow, and at the same time avoid a drop in the quality measurement of the student body were faced with the need for a fresh approach to marketing.

QUALITY, PRICE, AND RESULTANT VALUE

The American public is having great difficulty affording the cost of higher education. The mind-set that price guarantees quality is no more. The standard of living in the United States is decreasing, the need for an educated citizenry is increasing, and the public is demanding value in the delivery of education. In a sophisticated free market environment, maximum quality at minimum price determines value. The first institutions to recognize this emerging phenomenon and address the need will be the winners.

Quality programs, and the consultants to initiate the programs, are sweeping the country. Unfortunately, it required a competitive international market to make the U.S. wake up to its poor quality habits. Delivery of a quality product or service to the customer is easy. We are all customers and know what we want. Quality is a mixture of common sense and good management. Within a few short years, higher education will identify quality requirements, set up routine management procedures to fulfill quality standards, and retain professional management personnel to ensure that quality is a "way of life."

Price is going to be the difficult part of the formula. This book is dedicated to organizing the myriad of opportunities to reduce costs in order to offer affordable tuition to the public. In *Productivity and Higher Education*, edited by Richard E. Anderson and Joel W. Meyerson, the various authors meticulously outline all the entrenched reasons why it will be a difficult task to convince management and the faculty to do more (and better) with less. Unfortunately for the industry of higher education it will have to change the way business is organized and managed to survive in a new, highly competitive marketplace— a survival of the fittest.

PRODUCT OFFERINGS

In Chapter 6, we reviewed the need for cost systems in higher education. A cost system will make it possible for management to evaluate its academic offerings from a marketing/margin vantage point.

In a downsizing mode, the margin realized on various offerings will be essential to protect the financial viability of the institution as relative revenue flow diminishes. Part of any marketing strategy should consider deliberately changing marketing emphasis between programs to maximize margin opportunity. For example, if the per seat margin of the evening undergraduate school is less than the per seat margin of the evening graduate school, it would be wise to shift more of the marketing expenditures from the undergraduate to the graduate school if it is determined that the graduate school market can be penetrated.

Another example of effective downsizing would be the elimination of programs that lose money, have no relationship with other programs, and do not disturb the mission of the institution. In this example, eliminate all direct costs including marketing expense and faculty.

PARTIAL SUBSTITUTION OF OLDER, NONTRADITIONAL STUDENTS

Many institutions were convinced initially that they could recoup the loss of revenues from the full-time traditional day student with expanded part-time, nontraditional evening adult student programs. Several facts suggest, however, that increasing market share of evening students alone cannot provide the needed funds. For instance:

- To earn revenue equal to that of traditional enrollments, a nontraditional program requires far more students and associated services (i.e., seats, classrooms, parking, etc.). Classrooms and other facilities are finite. Expanding facilities to accommodate evening students without establishing a commensurate need for those facilities in the daytime is not financially feasible.
- The margin between gross revenues and expenses at many institutions is not as great for evening students as it is for day students. Nontraditional evening student tuition rates are set low because facilities are already available. Evening tuition rates should be increased to provide a greater margin and a partial offset to the loss of day revenues. (It is possible that the exponential rate of financial aid discounting to make an education affordable for the traditional full-time day student might drive day seat margins down to the point where there is more margin in the evening school, where financial aid discounting is only in the discussion stage.)
- If one accepts the above two points, there is a marketing opportunity. Integrate the evening undergraduate programs with their respective full-time day schools, charge the same course rate, and give the students and faculty the flexibility of compressing their school week. Although there may be some loss of evening enrollment, it might offer improved faculty utilization, reduced wear and tear on the facilities, and increased margin for the institution. In addition, the flexibility factor may attract students and faculty who desire the school week compression option. (Maintaining a desired level of nontraditional evening students could be achieved with selected use of tuition discounting for financial aid.)

HISTORICAL MARKETING IN HIGHER EDUCATION

Most institutions of higher education evolved without benefit of a formal marketing program supported by a plan outlining mission and market niche. Like any business, their marketplace was established by how the market perceived their product. The reputation of an institution feeds on itself. An institution with a growing reputation for quality attracts top faculty, and top faculty in combination with a quality curriculum attract the best students. Development of an institution in this evolutionary manner creates a natural dichotomy regarding reputation for quality. Does a quality faculty and curriculum provide a quality education for development of a quality student, or does a quality student come into an institution and acquire a quality education because the student will see to his or her own education under any set of circumstances? Although the issue is not clear-cut, the fact remains that an institution wants to attract both a quality faculty and a quality student body. Fortunately, many institutions that had runaway cost and the added burden of supporting major research programs were able to support their lifestyle with extraordinary tuition increases. These institutions were also fortunate because the public associated higher price with quality and stood in line to attend.

Institutions are taking marketing much more seriously than they did prior to 1985. The first step in a program to improve marketing is to understand the different relationships on campus, for example, that between the admission offices of the various schools and colleges within the institution, the activities and outreach of the faculty and management, as well as the formal public relations program of the institution. If an institution wants to be identified in a specific manner, it must have a coordinated program to define that image and see that all outreach brochures, advertising, and marketing project that image in the marketplace. Certain institutions have recognized this need and have established an "Enrollment Management" function, which in many cases has been elevated to a deanship and, occasionally, a vice presidency. A partial solution! What we are defining is a marketing function supported by well-executed strategic planning. Figure 7.1 illustrates an organizational pyramid, which encloses the "marketing" function of higher education that must be addressed. The organization is capped by the mission of the institution, followed by a designated executive with primary marketing responsibilities. At the bottom of the pyramid are the building blocks of the various admission operations.

Whatever organization structure is adopted to deal with the marketing pyramid shown above, it must address the need for someone to be in charge of all marketing initiatives within the institution. Further, it must address the need for the designated person to recognize the inter-relationship of the

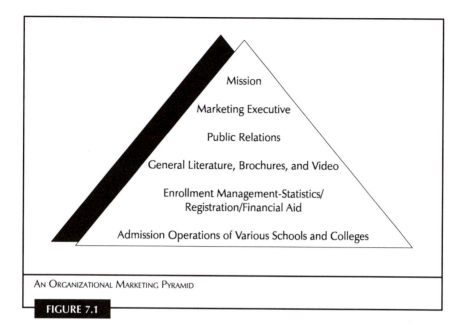

Mission

Marketing Executive

Public Relations

General Literature, Brochures, and Video

Enrollment Management-Statistics/
Registration/Financial Aid

Admission Operations of Various Schools and Colleges

AN ORGANIZATIONAL MARKETING PYRAMID

FIGURE 7.1

various segments of marketing and be responsible for the overall "marketing" budget. (Establishing a vice presidency for marketing was addressed in Chapter 2.)

FINDING A NICHE IN THE MARKETPLACE

The image and the marketing niche have to be designed around a societal need. As an example, hundreds of institutions provide degrees in business. If a college is to have a strong reputation in that field, both its undergraduate and graduate curricula have to be designed to provide the students with an education that is tailored to the current needs of industry. Following are examples for change to better market a business program to the marketplace that hires your students:

- Perhaps all students should have a sound understanding of accounting because that is the language of industry throughout the world.
- Perhaps the entire curriculum should be globalized to recognize that business is now an international arena.
- Perhaps all graduates should be computer literate and have the opportunity to use the computer in all disciplines within their curriculum because the use and application of computers in the business world is in its infancy.

- Perhaps industry prefers students with a broader base of education in the humanities coupled with their technical training.
- Perhaps the moral conduct of businesspeople today in our society is unacceptable and our young people require a sound foundation in ethics.
- Perhaps the faculty should be directed to work closely with industry to ensure that curriculum development and research are relevant.

Satisfy the students admitted to the institution, as well as the society and business world they enter upon graduation, and both customers will demand your product.

No amount of marketing or public relations is going to establish an enduring quality reputation for an institution. Quality will be judged primarily on the successes of the graduates and the professional reputations of the faculty members who are attracted to the institution. However, directing the advertising and public relations of the institution to highlight and place in perspective the performance of the faculty, and training received by the students, can only accelerate the development of a reputation. For an institution that has decided to change direction, using these same techniques will force a faster market perception of that change.

In addition to strategic marketing ploys, there are traditional factors that influence the marketing of an institution to students and their parents. These include the following:

- **Net annual cost to the student and parent.** Tuition discounting for financial aid is widespread and forces an institution to charge higher rates for students who can and will pay full price in order to provide a lower net price to students who cannot afford the full cost of education. As the market situation worsens, it will become increasingly important that institutions manage a cost-effective operation and thereby maintain tuition rates that are affordable and competitive. There will always be the exceptional family where the student and his or her parents accept the "Mercedes Benz" view that translates high tuition into a guarantee of quality. (High cost does not guarantee quality, although it goes a long way in providing the opportunity to ensure quality. However, most families do not have the "Mercedes Benz" view, and it is from this group of students that most applications are going to come. See Chapter 14 for a discussion on strategy to be applied to the subject of net price for a student to attend an institution.)

- **Breadth of nonacademic activities and services provided.** Nonacademic activities and services provided to students are not only important to the marketing program of the institution but also to the happiness and well-being of students. This is particularly true with a large residential student body. A town inhabited almost exclusively by bright, hyperactive young people will need a broad selection of activities to keep them busy 16 hours a day. A comprehensive program of physical and intellectual activities is extremely important in attracting and retaining students. It is also necessary for their development as responsible citizens.

- **General condition of the physical facilities and the ambiance of the campus.** The physical plant, consisting of the grounds, the buildings, parking lots, athletic fields, and the landscaping that integrate them, is extremely important to marketing the institution. The campus is home to the faculty, staff, students, parents, and visitors for eight or more hours a day. However, it is home 24 hours a day to those students who reside on the campus. If you want a happy campus, make the living experience pleasing, aesthetically attractive, and a place the student wants to come to rather than leave.

  The physical plant of an institution of higher education presents a unique opportunity for facility planning because there are few businesses that unite the development of a product (the student) with the living environment. Successful mating of the working experience with the living experience is the strategy. Complicating the problem is the fact that what you do has to be accomplished to the satisfaction of your neighbors, who at times find it difficult living next door to a "town" occupied almost exclusively by rambunctious young people.

  Successful development of the physical plant requires great finesse in the town and gown area to appease "town fathers" (mothers) who are delighted to have an institution that will bring intellectual and business opportunities to their city—but resent an organization that does not pay what is perceived to be its fair share of municipal costs and that is absolved from many building codes that restrict others. Concern for your neighbors, the town or city in which you reside, and a continuous program of diplomacy to maintain strong town and gown relations is extremely important. Be a good neighbor. Give what you can to your neighbors and your fellow townspeople, and never surprise them. Make sure the hamlet in which your campus resides is aware that all constituencies on campus are comparable to year-round tourists. They spend lots of money and are not a threat to the townspeople's jobs. Everybody loves tourist business! It's just a matter of education and orientation—marketing.

- **Availability of housing, particularly on-campus housing.** In recent years, an increasing number of students and their parents have come to recognize that the undergraduate years should be a total life involvement experience. For this reason, there is tremendous pressure on institutions to provide housing, particularly on-campus housing, to enable students to experience their undergraduate years with residence as a lifestyle. In fact, housing requirements are so important that to not provide housing when it is requested is detrimental to marketing. If one institution does not provide a bed, a competing institution will and, in the process, get the customer.

- **Location of the institution.** Applicants and their parents are influenced to a great extent in the selection of an institution by its location, its setting within a college community, services, recreational opportunities, local and long-distance travel accommodations, etc. Unfortunately, relocating your institution is not practical. However, a marketing program that extols the best an area has to offer is important, and should be promoted.

- **The reputation of the institution within the field the student wishes to pursue.** A simple statement will suffice. Reputation in great part is how your two customers, the student and society, perceive your institution. Perception is reality to the one perceiving, thus marketing is becoming more important in higher education for molding reputation.

Today's higher education market has provided a benefit to one group of our citizenry. The academically weak student without financial resources may have more opportunity not only to attend an institution of higher education but, in many cases, to enjoy a broad selection of campuses. This opportunity was born when institutions lowered their quality standards as a trade-off against allowing their revenue flow to drop below a manageable level.

Marketing has become so critical to higher education that, at the very least, it should be coordinated, possibly consolidated, with a central admissions/ enrollment management/public relations function, and its organization positioning should be reviewed. Marketing in higher education is becoming less polite and promises to become more rough and tumble like it is in the industrial world. Most institutions will survive, some will thrive, and some will be discontinued, or absorbed, by other institutions. For sure, the management of higher education will change dramatically by the turn of the century, and those institutions that are well managed, develop an effective marketing program, and use strategic planning to influence their destiny will be stronger as a result.

In conclusion, marketing in a highly competitive marketplace is new to higher education. To be effective, it is going to require more attention, more money, an integrated approach, and more professional programs. Institutions that do not change will, in all likelihood, lose in the marketplace. Some institutions that do change will make mistakes and also lose in the marketplace. Whatever change is necessary, professional management people will find it to be an interesting challenge.

FOR FURTHER READING

Kotler, Philip, and Fox, Karen F. *Strategic Marketing for Educational Institutions.* Englewood Cliffs, NJ: Prentice-Hall, Inc., 1985.

Litten, Larry H.; Sullivan, Daniel; and Brodigan, David L. *Applying Market Research in College Admissions.* New York: College Entrance Examination Board, 1983.

Paulsen, Michale B. *College Choice: Understanding Student Enrollment Behavior.* ASHE-ERIC Higher Education Report no. 6. Washington, DC: The George Washington University, School of Education and Human Development, 1990.

PART
IV

· · · · · · · · ·

Revenue Sources

CHAPTER 8

·········

Tuition, Auxiliary Enterprises, and Other Revenue Opportunities

igher education has many sources of revenue. However, the primary source, particularly at nonresearch institutions, has and will continue to be tuition. The dependence of institutions on tuition makes higher education vulnerable to a decline in student enrollment. This chapter is devoted to increased development of other revenue sources.

Other revenue sources can produce at least a break-even financial arrangement and, in most cases, an excess (with the exception of research, which frequently is a financial drain on an institution). Endowment income does not always provide a direct revenue source to the institution. Endowments set up as scholarships are funds given to students to pay their tuition and other costs and do not provide direct relief to the institution in the form of revenue or cost displacement. However, they provide indirect financial support because they allow the institution to target student diversity. Gifted students and financial need students are recruited who would probably attend another institution and adversely affect budgeted enrollment and revenue levels.

SOURCES OF REVENUE

This chapter reviews the following:

- Tuition
- Fees
- Room
- Board
- Athletic and other related or unrelated educational activities

- Research and grants
- Endowment income
- Income from working capital
- Annual giving
- Gifts-in-kind
- Rental of facilities to external organizations
- Excess revenues

Tuition

Tuition is the fee charged for instruction and all direct and indirect costs associated with the education process. It is the primary source of revenue in higher education and is paid, in whole or in part, by all students, with the exception of those few who are on a full scholarship granted by the institution or a third party. (Scholarships and financial aid are detailed in Chapter 14.) Because tuition is the largest source of revenue at most institutions, the amount paid is usually established at the time annual budgets are prepared, after all other sources of revenue are determined. Unfortunately, for the public, tuition at most institutions has been a cost-plus business with the rate being determined on the basis of the need of the institution, relative to what the market will bear. Extraordinary annual increases in tuition rates started at the time inflation reached double-digit proportions in the late 1970s and have been perpetuated until recently by the spiraling costs of education, in combination with declining demographics, which together are creating serious financial problems for the education industry. Tuition is the great financial equalizer. The difference in revenues required to maintain the institution at a break-even level is derived from tuition.

Fees

Fees are not usually a major source of income and because of their association with tuition are usually lumped under the umbrella category "Tuition and Fees Revenue." Students attending a public institution would take exception to this practice because fees have become a substantial portion of their cost as state institutions scramble to provide an income as an offset to declining tax income subsidy. Fees take the form of ancillary costs to tuition. Fees are separated from tuition because they are not charged to all students. Examples would be lab fees, graduation fees, and parking.

Conversely, a fee that is applicable to all students would be a student affairs fee or a computer support fee. Unfortunately, the separation of a fee that is applicable to all students from the basic tuition rate is a deception because it makes the common tuition rate of the institution appear lower than the actual rate. This deception became widespread during the 1980s as institutions aggressively increased their tuition rates, upsetting the public. The strategy was to make it difficult for students and their parents to calculate an equitable comparison of gross institution cost from information contained in the brochures of competing institutions.

Room

Residency in higher education has increasingly become a way of life as students and their parents seek to combine the education process with the living experience. Resident accommodations take on many forms, from an individual living by himself or herself in an apartment to a group of two to four students sharing a single dorm room. No matter what the variations between these two extremes (including townhouses), the ultimate difference is the eating arrangement. If the facilities include kitchen accommodations, then the student is living in what is designated as an apartment compared to facilities that do not provide private dining areas and require the students to eat in a central resident dining room. With the advent of the whole life experience in recent years, apartments have become more popular than dorm facilities.

Apartment-style living, with kitchen facilities and independent bathrooms, are more expensive to construct but also can be rented at a rate that absorbs the higher cost. It is still a good idea to maintain dorm style living for freshmen to provide a transition from dependence on their family at home to total independence within an apartment.

Apartment accommodations offer capacity advantages to the institution. From a facility utilization point of view, apartments offer the flexibility of accommodating students either on a dorm arrangement, whereby they are fed in the resident dining areas, or the independence of an apartment. Dormitory accommodations without kitchen facilities and independent bathrooms do not provide this type of flexibility. In addition, apartments, during a period of reduced demand for resident accommodations, can be rented, leased, or sold to third parties, particularly if they are on the peripheral edge of the campus or, better yet, off campus. Apartments also offer more flexibility for rental during the summer.

Other advantages of apartment accommodations include the flexibility of housing students during Christmas shutdown, holidays, between semesters, and during the summer months when it is difficult if not unprofitable to provide centralized food service in the dining halls. This will become more important as institutions recruit internationally, increasing the number of students enrolled for whom it is not practical to return home during the periods mentioned. Finally, apartments require less custodial support and instill pride in the students because the accommodations are more homey than a communal living arrangement in a dorm.

The beginning of a cost-effective housing program, which will allow for significant margins to be generated, is initiated at the time of construction. Facilities should be designed for minimal material required for construction, ease of construction, minimum maintenance, maximum energy efficiency, and appropriate aesthetics to maintain morale and enhance the opportunity to charge higher room rates.

Pricing rooms would be extremely difficult if doing so was predicated solely on the many cost variables that should, or should not, influence the relative difference in rates between rooms. Instead, allow student demand for the various facilities to be your primary means of establishing rate variances between accommodations. The most efficient means of determining a demand response is the use of a lottery each year when rooms are assigned. A lottery determines which rooms are the most popular and, therefore, prices can be set accordingly. The secondary purpose of a lottery is to stop the continual churning of room changes that result from discontent. If prices are in balance with demand, the students will settle down because the lottery provides a balance between desire and ability to pay.

Board

Board is the food service for resident students. Not all resident students require a board program. It is expected that most students housed in apartment accommodations will prepare their own meals. Board plans are usually set up with a variation of meal plans. They can run the gamut from 5 meals a week up to 19, depending on personal eating habits and lifestyle.

The costing and pricing of meal plans is an exercise in statistical probability. Costing is based on the expected number of meal plans that will be purchased under the various arrangements, the number of meals consumed against the individual plans, and the cost of food for the various options.

Institutional food service can be subcontracted (outsourced), or the institution can manage its own program. If the program is outsourced, the institution's opportunity to realize a margin on the program will be the spread between the costs charged by the subcontractor to the institution and the price passed on to the students. The subcontractor will expect to make at least 5 percent on its total cost. This figure seems low. However, it should be noted that the subcontractor has (1) a minimal investment in the operation, (2) an opportunity for intra-divisional markup on food before costing to the institutions, and (3) an opportunity to choose corporate "overhead." Considerable room for development of hidden subcontractor profit if not subjected to periodic competitive bid.

In those situations where the institution runs an in-house program, there is the opportunity to realize a margin on the full range between costs incurred and the price passed on to the student. Unless all students are on a food plan and housed by the institution, however, management must maintain some balance on margins derived from tuition, fees, room, and board. It would be unfair to the resident students if inordinate margins realized by the institution were on room and board as opposed to tuition—a common margin source. Unfortunately, institutions break even or lose money on education programs and realize their margins on ancillary programs.

Athletic and Other Related or Unrelated Educational Activities

Ancillary activities for athletics and other ventures bring visibility and revenue to an institution. They may be related, or unrelated, to the not-for-profit mission of the institution, and they may, or may not, support their cost. These ancillary activities can include varsity athletic programs, research centers, hospitals, hotels, and golf courses.

An example of a related, versus unrelated, activity would be a hotel. If the institution has a hotel management program and students in the program operate the facility without profit, it is related. If the hotel is operated independently of the institution, it is unrelated, and should be incorporated as a for-profit entity. Under this arrangement, ownership percentage retained by the institution will determine what proportion of profit after tax can be transferred back to the institution.

Research and Grants

Sponsored research and grants are a complicated and troublesome source of revenue. If an institution and its faculty have the ambition to do more than teach students, they will be encouraged to migrate into sponsored research and grants. Research is a necessary part of scholarly activity and serves the purposes of (1) allowing faculty members to maintain an edge in their fields, (2) attracting top faculty, (3) providing prestigious recognition for the institution, and (4) contributing to society's needs.

Sponsored research is performed by faculty who prepare proposals to industrial, commercial, educational, and governmental organizations. The contract grantor, in effect, buys the time of the individual faculty member, which absolves the professor from all or part of the assigned teaching load. In addition, most government contractors will pay a portion of an overhead rate that has been prenegotiated by an appropriate government agency. The overhead rate that is negotiated includes most, but not all, of the costs associated with supporting an institution. Industry and most foundations, however, take the position that indirect costs are already absorbed by the institution and, therefore, they should pay only directly assignable costs.

Grants are a more generous form of revenue. They take the form of funds provided individual academic departments for research work in their field, purchase of equipment, or support of programs. A grant is a generous gift because the initiative would be paid by the institution if the grant were not provided.

Endowment Income

Endowment income provides many variations of subsidy to current operations. Unfortunately, few of them are a direct subsidy to operations. The income from most endowments provides for a richer academic and scholarly environment but does not pay for the day-to-day expenses of running the institution. The forms that these endowments take are scholarship monies credited to the students' accounts, faculty enrichment funds to provide unusual enhancements for the faculty, faculty chairs that do not necessarily relieve the teaching load on the institution, and cultural programs for the student body, faculty, and administration.

Endowments that do provide relief to operations are not very attractive to givers; they are limited to funding such things as the upkeep of facilities, purchase of capital equipment, and other unglamorous operation expenditures. Institutions that receive operation endowments are fortunate and should find themselves less tuition dependent.

An endowment that is even better than the operation endowment is the quasi-endowment. Quasi-endowments are institutional funds working as an endowment. The quasi-funds are derived from unrestricted gifts that management has decided to retain rather than spend immediately, excess revenues from operations, and accumulated earnings on the quasi-endowment funds. Many institutions will summarize quasi-endowments, including fund balances and reserves, within the Endowment and Similar Funds budget category to give the institution a strong balance sheet appearance. In addition, consolidating unrestricted funds within the Endowment and Similar Funds provides a larger endowment per student calculation when applying for a bond issue.

The board of trustees may authorize management to use the principal and income within the quasi-endowment fund to make extraordinary acquisitions, to relieve current operation expenditures, or to designate an annual transfer of funds from the quasi-endowment via a spending formula for subsidizing current operations.

Quasi-endowments are management's most coveted form of capital because there are no legal restrictions on the use of the funds for support of the institution, and no offsetting debt. Annual giving and income from investment of quasi-endowments/working capital are the only forms of revenues against which there are no required expenditures or other quid pro quo commitment. Institutions that accumulate a large portion of their endowments in the form of quasi-endowments have the opportunity to become less tuition dependent. Benefactors of the institution should be encouraged to give unrestricted funds that can either be used for current operations or added to the quasi-endowment. In addition, management should be encouraged to incur excess revenues on a regular basis to accumulate quasi-endowments for reinvestment in the institution at a later time.

Income from Working Capital

In addition to endowment funds that are invested and provide an income, a not-for-profit institution also has working capital like any other business. Fortunately for higher education, its primary sources of revenue—tuition, fees, room, and board—are received in two extraordinary amounts twice a year, before each semester. The institution will invest these revenue funds while they are expended over the next six months. This is unlike most businesses, which operate on a hand-to-mouth basis with monthly revenues offset in great part by monthly expenditures. With judicial investment on a short-term basis against a well-managed cash flow program, an institution can realize an appreciable sum of income from investment of short-term capital funds.

Annual Giving

Annual giving is the quintessential form of institution revenue. It is unrestricted monies given for current operations, with no "strings" attached. Because the money is given without restrictions, instead of in the form of a restricted gift or an endowment, the entire sum can be used to support current operations. Although some friends of the institution and industry might provide annual giving, it is derived primarily from alumni. Annual giving should be encouraged not only because it is a wonderful form of operational revenue but because it gets alumni and others into the mode of recurring giving. Regular donors to annual giving frequently become major givers to capital campaigns and eventually may become involved in planned giving (deferred).

Gifts-in-Kind

There is a positive side, and a negative side, to gifts-in-kind and services. A desirable gift would be a facility, equipment, or service that the institution desperately needs and would eventually have to spend its own money to acquire. The gift of a much-needed building relieves the institution of the debt service for construction of the building, if funds are to be borrowed, or an extraordinary reduction in quasi-endowments to finance the acquisition. The negative side is the institution may not have a strong need for the type of gift granted and perhaps should be more selective in what it accepts, unless the gift can be sold at a later date. An undesirable gift could take the form of a facility that is infrequently used and forces the institution to incur an ongoing maintenance cost that was not included as an endowment in the original gift.

Another form of giving that is similar to gifts-in-kind is an in-part gift to a project. Using a building again as an example, if a capital campaign project is established for the construction of a new building, and many benefactors give, in part, toward that building, the gifts are not retained in an endowment but reduce the funding required to construct the building. Specifically, these partial gifts reduce debt service, or reduce the amount that must be paid from current operations, or quasi-endowment, or reduce all three sources of construction payment.

Rental of Facilities to External Organizations

Financial pressures on higher education management are mounting, and institutions are becoming much more aggressive in using available facilities to derive revenues from third parties who will pay for services rendered. These services include rental of facilities with food and overnight accommodations for conferences, seminars, athletic camps, etc. As higher education becomes more aggressive in this area, the government will become more concerned about an institution using its tax-exempt properties for profit purposes.

The government recognizes that certain third-party ventures are related to the education mission of the institution and accepts these revenue sources within the not-for-profit charter of the institution. However, activities that are not related to the purpose of its tax-exempt status must be identified as taxable ventures, and appropriate revenue and expenditures must be summarized to determine if there is profit subject to tax. An institution also has to be careful of its property tax situation with regard to the city, state tax requirements, and unfair competition complaints from local vendors.

Related and unrelated third-party activities provide a lucrative opportunity to generate margins that can be used to offset tuition needs. Facilities are available on weekends and, to a great extent, during the summer months. There are even times during the day when various classrooms, conference rooms, and eating facilities are available for rent to organizations that are having a conference or some other education-related function. With declining enrollment, more excess capacity will be made available during the 1990s, including classroom and residential accommodations during the academic year. Real costs are minimal because the fixed costs of the facilities have already been absorbed by the institution. Somewhere between competitive pricing and the variable costs of providing the facilities at the institution is a price that is attractive to the customer and provides a handsome revenue/ margin to the institution. The whole area of conferencing and special events should be aggressively pursued by all institutions of higher education, while being sensitive to (1) the convenience of students or faculty, (2) possible tax requirements, and (3) the best interest of local vendors.

Excess Revenues

A not-for-profit organization is compelled to generate revenues in excess of expenditures from current operations. It is a capital opportunity that should be planned for and budgeted to be accomplished. Over the long term, it reduces pressure on tuition by providing an offset to expense requirements in the future, capital for cost reduction opportunities, and financing for expansion of programs and facilities. Excess revenues are reviewed further in Chapter 15.

SEGREGATION OF REVENUE SOURCES

Having listed the many revenue sources for an institution, it is necessary to understand the differences between the sources and why they are segregated into academic operations and auxiliary enterprises.

All revenues and expenditures for operations are summarized under one fund, referred to as the current fund. However, they are segregated between academic revenues and expenditures, and auxiliary enterprise revenues and expenditures. The reason for the separation is twofold: (1) An institution of higher education for commuter students can theoretically operate without auxiliary enterprises, and (2) auxiliary enterprises are the business side of a not-for-profit entity. Auxiliary enterprises provide a home, entertainment, counseling, and a social life for the students, primarily the resident students. The institution could be a commuter arrangement where students come to the classroom, learn, and go home. In this situation, an institution would have to survive on its tuition and fees, research, and other forms of gifts. However, all institutions, to varying degrees, provide auxiliary enterprises for the student body. The many functions in this category are ancillary to the academic mission of the school and provide an opportunity to generate revenues that can be used to subsidize that academic mission.

Room and board are the traditional auxiliary enterprises of an institution, and both can be priced on a competitive basis: competitive to off-campus opportunities and competitive to similar institutions in the same locality.

As has been emphasized throughout this book, higher education is a complicated business. There is a purpose for higher education's not-for-profit status and exemption from taxes, but there is also a responsibility that higher education be operated by business managers who can live within the definition of what is not-for-profit, maximize cost-efficiency opportunities, maximize revenue enhancement opportunities, strive for quality in administration and instruction, and, in the process, satisfy a societal need at a price the American public can afford.

CHAPTER 9

Fund Raising and Grants

A major factor in ensuring the success of an institution of higher education is its ability to raise third-party funds. If an institution is not aggressive in its fund-raising program, it will be limited primarily to revenues received from tuition; other forms of student support, such as room, board, and athletics; and research. This chapter reviews the many types of funds that can be raised, the purpose of each, and the strategies in approaching various sources of funding. As mentioned in the introduction to this book, a not-for-profit organization can receive support from tax-exempt gifts, however, this chapter will not review the tax implications and tax strategies associated with such gifts.

TYPES OF SOURCES

There are five basic types of giving to an institution.

- Current gifts, including annual giving, unrestricted gifts, real estate, buildings, capital equipment, and services
- Scholarship endowments
- General endowments
- Planned gifts
- Grants

Each of these funding forms eventually flows into operations, or relieves spending; each has varying effects on the success of an institution.

Current Gifts

All current gifts, including annual giving, real property, and services, affect operations. For this reason, they are accounted immediately to either operations or as an asset to the property fund rather than accumulated as an endowment.

Annual giving or unscheduled unrestricted gifts are cash receipts from alumni and friends of the institution given to management to be spent for whatever purpose best serves the current needs of the institution. Unrestricted gifts, whether they be designated for current use or unrestricted as to timing of expenditure, are the form of giving most appreciated by management. Alumni are encouraged to start annual giving as soon as they graduate. It is hoped that their giving will evolve into a lifetime annual commitment and increase as their fortunes develop. In addition, it is recognized that people who give annually are in basic agreement with management and the direction of the institution and, therefore, provide an excellent candidate base for major gifts at a later date, or possibly throughout their lifetime.

Many institutions, both private and public, were originally started at the time our republic was conceived by means of land grants originally from the king and later from both the federal government and individual states. The gift of real estate is generally much encouraged, particularly land that is contiguous to a campus or has value for resale or development at a later date. However, land and other property must have real value to the institution. Land with potential access or environmental problems should be examined, and certainly an institution does not want obsolete equipment.

Buildings can be given as an existing structure, or even better, in total or in part by an individual for a purpose, and on a site designated by the administration. Many buildings are given as a whole, or in part, during capital campaigns when management has defined its needs for particular structures. In other cases, benefactors will provide a building for a function or operation they feel is important, even though management has not designated such a desired gift. An example of this might be a theater, performing arts auditorium, or museum. These are welcome gifts for programs that remain elusive during periods of financial restraint. However, an institution should avoid accepting a structure gift that requires upkeep expense in excess of practical usage.

Today, fewer buildings are being constructed because of existing excess capacity. Many facility needs are being satisfied by modifying existing structures. Institutions with existing structures that have not been named after a benefactor should covet these structures for fund-raising purposes. Benefactors may be convinced to give money for an existing structure to be named in their honor. The benefit of this approach is that such benefactors can be asked to make their gifts unrestricted, allowing the college to use the funds for current operations.

Gifts of capital items and services are also appreciated. If the equipment is in good condition and its use is required, or the services are needed by the institution, management can substitute these gifts for items that would normally be in the operating budget. Equipment and services are difficult gifts to solicit, in any significant amount, because they lack the immortality opportunity offered by endowments and buildings bearing the benefactor's name. The ideal benefactors are those who hold the philosophy "Blessed are those who give in the best interest of the institution as directed by management."

Endowments

The types of giving we have discussed so far under the broad category of gifts do not result in what is traditionally identified as endowments. As previously mentioned, gifts are either consumed in current operations, or they are established within the physical plant accounting and merged with other capital items acquired by the institution. Endowments, on the other hand, represent the accumulated wealth of many individuals, organizations, and foundations that have provided a principal balance to be established permanently, with an income flow in perpetuity, to be used by the administration as determined by the benefactor. Institutions with major endowments have more independence and financial flexibility than do institutions that are dependent almost entirely on student-related revenues. Endowments are unique to the not-for-profit sector and are extremely complicated from a financial point of view.[1] For this reason, we will discuss the many forms of endowments in some depth.

Endowments can be restricted or unrestricted regarding both principal and earnings. The disposition of a restricted endowment is entirely at the direction of the benefactor. The benefactor can direct that all, or a part, of the earnings be used for a specific purpose. In certain circumstances, he or she may direct that the earnings, plus a part of the principal, be used as long as the principal balance is sufficient to support a fixed expenditure dictated by the benefactor. Certainly an endowment should serve the needs of the institution in some constructive manner. If a proposed endowment does not serve the best interest of the institution, management should attempt to convince the benefactor to change the directed purpose of the expenditures.

Restricted endowments take two forms: (1) those that directly support operations such as endowment of a faculty chair, faculty development, re-

---

[1]For further reading on endowment management, refer to William F. Massy, *Endowment Perspectives, Policies, & Management* (Washington, DC: Association of Governing Boards of Universities and Colleges, 1990).

search, building maintenance, or services; and (2) those that indirectly support current operations such as scholarships for the student body. A restricted endowment can support any expenditure necessary to run the institution. One may wish to set up an endowment to support the cost of maintaining a first-class faculty or to subsidize physical plant operations. Other forms of endowments are those that support named professorships in a discipline that is of particular interest to the benefactor or those that establish programs for cultural development for the student body or the faculty. Also included within restricted endowments are planned gifts, at least for the interim period until the institution receives the proceeds of the principal, which may or may not be continued as an endowment depending on directed disposition of funds upon the death of the benefactor.

The best known form of restricted endowments are funds established for scholarships to support students. This form of support to an institution has an indirect impact on current operations, which is difficult to measure until endowments of this form become a substantial portion of financial aid for students. Support is termed indirect because the endowment is not given for current operations to defray internal spending but rather for the students to help them pay their tuition, room, board, and other expenses. If such students were to find the funds elsewhere to attend the institution, the institution does not necessarily benefit by this giving. However, in most instances, this form of support to the students does make a difference if it influences the students' decision to attend and if their enrollment is necessary to achieve the revenue budget. As mentioned, if the endowments for scholarships become substantial, they should reduce the level of tuition discounting for financial aid and conserve institution funds. Tuition discounting is discussed in Chapter 14.

An unrestricted endowment is a fund acting as an endowment. However, the principal and the earnings are both disposable at the discretion of the administration. Unrestricted endowments are commonly referred to as quasi-endowments. The sources of funds for accumulating quasi-endowments are gifts from friends who realize that management may have a need of such funds at a later date, excess revenues accumulated from current operations for which there is no immediate need, and earnings on the investment of quasi-endowment funds, including realized gains. By a vote of the board of trustees, the institution can use the earnings from quasi-endowments or the principal for current needs if required. In addition to annual giving, the earnings on quasi-endowments can provide a primary source of nonstudent-related cash flow to the institution if the earnings are transferred to current operations and spent the year of the transfer.

Planned Gifts

Planned gifts make up a quid pro quo form of giving that allows the institution to add the gift to the endowment fund and provide the benefactor with an income flow during his or her lifetime. The institution benefits by this form of gift upon the benefactor's death, at which time the principal is available to the institution. During the interim period, the institution benefits because the funds strengthen the balance sheet.

Planned gifts require a considerable amount of administration during the years the income is diverted to the benefactor. Although no one, to my knowledge, has determined the length of time that a planned gift can be administrated before the administrative costs exceed the value of the gift, it probably is not longer than the expected life of a middle-aged benefactor. Money has a value, determined by inflation and the earnings that can be realized on principal, which dictates that the longer a gift is deferred, the less value it has in current terms. An extreme example would be a planned gift established for a newborn female child today who will live to the age of 85. A million dollar gift today will have a value of approximately $1,000 in 85 years. This loss of value occurs because of inflationary devaluation of the dollar and loss of earnings opportunity to the institution on the investment. (The devaluation for inflation and earnings loss was calculated at 8 percent.)

Some balance to this "present value" phenomenon can be achieved by reducing the guaranteed earnings on the principal during the lifetime of the individual. For example, one could be generous and expand the income flow to as high as 12 percent for a gift received from an 80-year-old benefactor. Conversely, it would be smart to limit the income flow to 5 percent for a gift received from a 40-year-old alumnus who has a life expectancy of 80.

A major planned gift should always be reviewed carefully by the vice president of institutional advancement and the vice president of finance. It is possible to identify the many variables, including administrative cost, load them into a computer model, and do a computation considering present value and its implications relative to the value of the gift upon expected receipt. In the example above, where it was noted that the income for a young person should be as low as 5 percent, the institution would expect to do better than that on the investment of the principal and thereby accumulate additional principal during the life of the individual to compensate for inflation devaluation.

There is yet another variable that introduces risk regarding planned gifts. Suppose the institution decides not to invest the funds in a fixed-interest instrument that would provide an income at least sufficient to satisfy the guarantee made the benefactor. The institution may wish to invest the money in the stock market, an investment pool, or some other variable form of investment that may result in the institution losing a portion of principal. Another risk is to guarantee an income flow of 8 percent to an elderly person on a fixed-instrument investment paying 8 percent. If the benefactor lives beyond the maturity date and insists on a fixed-instrument investment, the institution might find itself reinvesting at a rate less than the 8 percent guaranteed life payment. In this example, the value of the gift would be depleted by inflation, and the institution would be obligated to a payment rate that exceeds earnings.

Management should make every attempt to convince those wishing to make a planned gift to allow the funds to be invested in the institution's asset allocation pool. This will provide the opportunity to earn more than the life income rate.

In spite of the many problems associated with planned giving, it is an excellent vehicle for transfer of wealth to the institution and should be developed. Because of the quid pro quo arrangement and the fact that the institution is, in effect, running a trust department to administer this type of giving, many people would not give in another form if there was not some arrangement that would benefit them during their lifetime. Planned giving is an investment in the future. When an institution first decides to administer this form of giving, it must realize that there is a long period of gestation before receipt of the funds. However, over the long term, when this form of giving program matures, there will be a steady flow of revenue in perpetuity.

Unfortunately, like many leaders in the business world, management in higher education is frequently oriented to short-term results. For this reason, some administrations are reluctant to make the initial investment in a planned giving program when they know that if effort devoted to planned giving was diverted to current giving, it would provide immediate results during their tenure, albeit, probably at a reduced level of giving, but at full present-day value.

Grants

Grants have been saved until last in this discussion of the various types of funds that can be raised because grants are a hybrid form of giving. One form of grant is a gift solicited by the institutional advancement organization from foundations and corporations to support various aspects of the institution, which usually stipulates that the funds will only be spent currently for a specific purpose. In some cases, grants are a joint venture between the institutional advancement organization and another operating division. In certain cases, a grant must be matched by the institution or other benefactors.

However, the form of grants most recognized in higher education that can develop into major programs are research grants solicited by the faculty. Research grants are sponsored and funded by government, industry, and foundations. Sponsored research grants serve as an excellent form of public relations; attract national or international recognition for the institution; attract and retain well-known and established faculty members; and, in many cases, provide an opportunity for an institution to pursue a new endeavor, new field, or new curriculum on a joint venture basis with an organization that has the same interests in mind. Most grants are structured to purchase a faculty member's time. This goal is achieved by reducing the teaching load for the faculty member to work in an area identified by government, industry, or a foundation as directly applicable to its needs, institutional needs, or a societal need. Collaborative ventures between small colleges could provide future revenue opportunities.

MANAGING A FUND-RAISING PROGRAM

The preceding has provided an overview of the various forms of major fund-raising opportunities in higher education. Next to be reviewed is the planning and coordination required to manage a comprehensive fund-raising program that is integrated into the day-to-day affairs of an institution; also examined are the long-range aspirations of such a program. In Chapter 4, revenue sources from fund raising were briefly reviewed. Strategic direction and planning for long-term development of an institution include a study of the many revenue sources available, or to be made available, to the institution. Although tuition and fees are the primary sources of revenue at most institutions of higher education, fund raising is a secondary source and must be integrated in a planned manner with other revenue sources. Fund raising will never be a serious endeavor unless it is thoughtfully planned and the chief officer and the board of trustees are charged with the mission of making it happen.

The first step in a fund-raising program is to determine current areas of potential funding and realistically assess what is possible in each area. The second step is to review the institution's strategic long-term plans to determine supplementary revenue sources required to complement tuition, room and board, and other sources of revenue available to the institution. If these two steps are not addressed, it is impossible to develop a cohesive, integrated approach to fund raising and capital campaigns.

Fund raising is a form of marketing sales, and as such, it requires years of cultivating customers who are willing to buy your product. The product, in this case, is the institution, its needs, and the willingness of the customer to support those efforts. The primary customers are the alumni of the institution and friends of the institution, which include individuals, foundations, corporations, and government agencies that have an interest in the institution and its success in areas they are willing to support. The board of trustees is a major part of the fund-raising efforts of the institution. It serves the dual role of assisting the development and management of its fund-raising and capital campaign programs, as well as serving as a primary source of funds, either directly or indirectly.

Board members are the fulcrum in a capital campaign because their selection, to a great extent, had been determined by what they could bring to the institution in the form of personal wealth, in addition to their network of contacts in support of the institution. If the board has not been properly selected and cultivated, fund raising will be difficult and will probably fall short of its goals or never realize potential goals because of this built-in handicap.

Capital campaigns frequently have a cycle of up to nine years. Successive campaigns will overlap each other in their various stages of development and execution. A campaign can be divided into three phases: (1) approximately two years for development and planning; (2) two years of accumulating a portion of the financial goal; and (3) approximately three to five years from public announcement of the campaign and its goal to successful completion. Momentum in the campaign is achieved during phase two by collection, or pledge, of 20 percent to 40 percent of the total campaign. This allows a public announcement that a successful campaign is under way. Early apparent success helps to encourage all who are, or will be associated with the campaign.

After the institutional needs have been identified and financial goals set to meet them, the vice president of institutional advancement should work with the chief financial officer to coordinate an ideal cash flow requirement to ensure that the institution does not run a deficit or incur unnecessary debt during the planned term of the campaign. Their coordinated efforts support the financial base of the institution's strategic plan.

The administration should make every attempt to solicit the type of funds identified as an institutional need and determine their timing. Realistically, however, a considerable portion of the funds raised will result from what interests the givers, rather than what is necessarily a planned need of the institution. If the board of trustees has the security of a quasi-endowment that it can spend at its discretion, the hiatuses in cash flow can be weathered by temporarily using quasi-endowment funds for development of projects. For instance, if a building is required for expansion of a new program, for which campaign funding is not fully solicited, the board of trustees could authorize the administration to borrow from quasi-endowment funds for construction of the building and replace the borrowed quasi-endowment funds with campaign proceeds at a later date. This decision would have to be weighed against the cost of an interim, or long-term, loan from a third party and the loss of earnings from the temporarily encumbered endowment funds.

For the purpose of providing current fund-raising operation, the initiation of a new campaign can be started in the last two years of the current five-year campaign. As mentioned previously, the first two years are a period of study, evaluation, and cultivation for the next campaign, and can be conducted quietly in parallel during the last two years of a current campaign. In this manner, five-year campaigns can be initiated two years after the wrap-up of the current campaign.

This approach not only allows for continuous fund raising as a revenue source but also permits the institution to maintain a capital campaign staff on an uninterrupted basis rather than hiring and firing fund raisers, which results in a program managed by professional gunslingers moving from organization to organization. Individuals moving from organization to organization are hardly the type of personnel you want to maintain the continuity of a long-term cultivation program.

Over the course of a campaign's nine-year life cycle, people, events, and needs will change. As such, the capital campaign must be flexible and continually readdress changing issues within the strategic plan of the institution. Fund flow needs can change, as can fund sources. A campaign's direction can be subtly changed without disturbing the public's view of the purpose and intent of a major campaign. The overriding issue of a campaign is the theme, which, if maintained in a broad sense, will allow for continuous fine tuning of the campaign thrust and direction.

In this era of runaway tuition rates, shrinking government support, and the ever-expanding requirements to provide a first-rate education for today's society, fund raising is taking on a new direction and is needed more than ever. As a result, capable professionals are moving into this sector. Their salaries are increasing commensurate with their skills and the growing importance of third-party giving to support education. Of primary focus in evaluating the performance of these professionals is the need to develop criteria that relate their fund-raising capacity to the resources they expend, preferably on a ratio basis for each area of funds: for instance, spend a dollar, raise 10 dollars.

Depending on the maturity of the organization, the seriousness with which its board of trustees addresses fund raising, and the experience of the chief fund raiser, the money spent for staff and expenses to raise funds should have a ratio of certainly no less than two dollars of funds raised for every dollar spent and, it is hoped, a ratio as high as 10 to 1.[2] An average acknowledged by the industry for a successful fund-raising program is 3–7 to 1 (after discounting deferred gifts).

Fund raising has always been a challenge, particularly for institutions that have realized excesses from operations, which is most institutions of higher education. Why most? Because most institutions do not raise sufficient funds from development sources to make an appreciable difference in the financing of current operations. An institution can not develop and grow on debt financing alone, and therefore most institutions, over time, generate excesses from operations that are reinvested in facilities, personnel, and programs. Fund accounting is designed for accountants to make excesses, necessary for growth, difficult to track through carefully executed "transfers between funds." Such tactics may be fun and games, but they are absolutely necessary to avoid the appearance of a "profit" in the legislated not-for-profit business sector, while serving the second purpose of avoiding explanations to would-be givers as to why they should be generous to an organization that makes a profit. (The shortcomings of the not-for-profit designation will be addressed in Chapter 15.)

It is of paramount importance that management explain to potential givers the reasons why it is necessary that higher education be financed by gifts, in addition to debt financing and the reinvestment of what are euphemistically called "profits." If giving was important when higher education was realizing operation excesses, it will become critical in the future, when deficit operations are widespread.

Important reasons for giving that should be conveyed to the public include:

- Opportunity in the 1990s to help the most important industry in the United States remain financially viable, contain costs to avoid excluding academically qualified students from attaining an education, and remain economically competitive in a global society.
- Opportunity to give back to society and achieve "15 minutes of immortality," yearly, if the endowment supports a scholarship or named professorship.
- Opportunity to have direct influence on how the monies they provide are spent by management.
- Opportunity to subsidize the cost of a societal mission and make education affordable to a larger number of citizens.

Third-party giving has always been critical but will mean survival for many institutions in the next decade.

---

[2] James L. Fisher and Gary H. Quehl, *The President and Fund Raising* (Phoenix, AZ: Oryx Press, 1989), 158-59.

The direction and packaging of third-party giving will have to change to address an industry that is in a downsize mode. The need will be to shift giving from operational needs, such as buildings and facilities, to annual giving, scholarships, and unrestricted gifts.

RECOMMENDED TACTICS

1. Sell the need for stepping up annual giving to support operations in order to reduce pressure to annually increase tuition.
2. Sell the need for scholarship endowments to directly support students in order to reduce the pressure of financial aid discounts on tuition increases.
3. Sell an aggressive planned giving program because it is a means of raising money by taking advantage of retirement tax laws. It appeals to those potential givers who are not totally motivated to give for benevolent reasons. Everybody wins; make the investment.
4. Sell existing unnamed buildings; they are a treasure. Seek commemorative gifts for existing buildings or common facilities. Funds for current operations can be raised by providing immortality opportunities in large bronze lettering.
5. Sell alumni on the principle that the not-for-profit business sector of higher education requires operation margin to survive, in addition to financing arrangements and the benevolence of its alumni and friends. Alumni and other potential donors are confused regarding the need for their support to an organization that appears to be "profitable." Convince your alumni that a profitable institution is more productive and will make their gift go further.

The importance of the board of trustees, and particularly its chairperson, to a successful fund-raising program has been stressed. However, if one is to identify the individual in an organization who is absolutely key, it would be the chief officer, whatever his or her title. The chief officer cannot be involved in every individual gift closing. However, it would be expected that the chief officer court major givers. Keep in mind that sales has its humbling side, because sales are based on outreach, which requires that the chief officer accommodate the giver in a variety of ways, including the arrangement of meeting places and times.

When it comes to fund raising, you win some and you lose some. A chief officer has to learn to live with rejection and play the statistics like everybody else in the marketing business. As in all business enterprises, everything eventually comes around to the chief officer as being the focal point for success.

FOR FURTHER READING

Kurzig, Carol M. *Foundation Fundamentals: A Guide for Grantseekers.* New York: The Foundation Center, 1980.

Lefferts, Robert. *The Basic Handbook of Grants Management.* New York: Basic Books, Inc., 1983.

Locke, Lawrence F.; Spirduso, Woneen Wyrick; and Silverman, Stephen J. *Proposals that Work: A Guide for Planning Dissertations and Grant Proposals.* Newbury Park, CA: Sage Publications, 1987.

CHAPTER 10

Investment Management

The methodology of investments and the willingness to take risk for the purpose of higher gain have changed significantly in higher education over the past 30 years. As is true of any business, higher education accumulates working capital from operating revenues net of expenditures that are available for temporary investment. In addition, higher education has the opportunity, and the mission, of accumulating both restricted and unrestricted funds in the form of endowments and reserves available for longer-term investment.

This chapter first reviews the two forms of investment opportunity in some detail for an understanding of why these funds are different in their need and, therefore, quite different when it comes to investment options. The two forms of capital for investment are working capital, which exists in all business, and endowment capital, which is unique to not-for-profit business (including higher education).

WORKING CAPITAL

Working capital is cash derived from running the business. Working capital is normally viewed on an annual cycle, and, from month to month, there are varying amounts available for temporary investment from operational cash flow. These types of funds are normally invested in certificates of deposit and U.S. treasury notes for 30- to 90-day periods, depending on projected cash requirements.

Higher education has an advantage in its opportunity to earn on the investment of working capital relative to other businesses. Tuition, room, and board, as mentioned previously, are normally paid during two periods of the year with most of the monies available for investment prior to the beginning of the academic semester. For this reason, the institution can invest these funds for a longer period of time relative to other businesses, which receive their income on a day-to-day or month-to-month basis. Investment of working capital, compared to longer-term opportunities in endowments, is relatively unsophisticated and entails no real risk. The instruments used for these investments are high grade with an assurance that the principal will be intact and a negotiated return will be paid for the invested period of time. The only real risk is that you may lose all or a part of the contractual interest if cash flow demands that an instrument be terminated before its maturity date.

The primary tool used for timing the investment of working capital is a well-developed cash flow model. The treasurer of an organization should project revenue receipts for the year and expected expenditures against the revenue flow. The model will disclose the varying amounts available to the institution on a monthly basis for investment. If the operation is not living on a hand-to-mouth basis and is able to invest available funds for anywhere from a month to three months or more, the treasurer will need to be aware of market circumstances affecting current and expected rates. The rule for short-term investments is simple: If you expect interest rates to go up in the near future, invest in short-term, 30-day notes or less, in order to continually take advantage of rising interest rates when the notes mature and are ready for reinvestment. If interest rates are expected to go down, invest at current rates for as long as possible in order to lock in the funds at the higher rate available at that time. The last step in the program of short-term investments is to arrange one or more lines of credit with banks to provide the option for short-term borrowing, which is sometimes necessary to avoid cashing in instruments that are close to maturity.

ENDOWMENT CAPITAL

A successful industrial business frequently has other funds besides working capital available for long-term investment if it is carrying reserves for unexpected eventualities, or accumulating funds for future ventures, such as an acquisition, major capital improvement, or repurchase of its stocks. However, it should be remembered that funds of this nature in industry belong to the stockholders, and if management can not demonstrate a plan for the eventual use of the funds, the stockholders may lobby to have them distributed as dividends or used to purchase outstanding stock. Higher education, on the other hand, is expected to accumulate funds in the form of restricted and unrestricted endowments and reserves to ensure an affordable tuition, and for operation of the institution in perpetuity. As a matter of fact, if an organization is successful, the endowments are expected to grow to whatever level of wealth the institution is capable of accumulating. Nobody owns a not-for-profit institution of higher education, and funds invested for future use serve to stabilize, as well as reduce, future tuition rate levels. Funds retained by higher education beyond immediate needs for working capital can be invested in longer-term instruments that may provide earnings in excess of those normally available on short-term working capital instruments.

CFO's Responsibilities for Endowment Management

The chief financial officer (CFO) is responsible for working with the board of trustees to ensure that clear policies exist concerning investment matters and spending rules governing the college's endowment. Balancing the need for current income with the goal of preserving the endowment in real terms for future generations is of primary importance. The CFO should also be instrumental in determining the college's position concerning the use of endowment funds to further various societal goals.

Investment Policy

The investment of long-term funds for endowments requires the CFO to carefully sort through the recommendations of economists, investment analysts, investment bankers, politicians, and soothsayers. The board of trustees will usually organize a subcommittee of the board of trustees, with members chosen according to their experience and ability to offer advice and counsel to the administration. The CFO reports to this committee.

The investment of endowment funds has changed significantly over the last 30 years. A heavy emphasis on conservatism used to be the overall policy exercised by trustees in carrying out their fiduciary duty. This policy arose from the concept that, as fiduciaries, they should not risk principal in the pursuit of higher return. There also was an expectation on the part of benefactors that funds would be invested in fixed-income instruments that would protect the principal balance.

Over the years, it became clear that investment policies maintaining funds in fixed-income investments did not provide sufficient earnings for both endowment spending and appreciation to offset the effect of inflation on the purchasing power of the principal balance. Consequently, the endowment was being maintained in nominal terms but was being eroded in inflation-adjusted terms. Generally, a proper balance between spending and reinvestment for inflation is met by the following equation:

TOTAL RETURN = SPENDING + INFLATION

TOTAL RETURN	=	earnings in the form of interest, dividends, and capital appreciation;
SPENDING	=	the amount distributed for scholarships or other college purposes; and
INFLATION	=	the inflation index for higher education.

For example, if the principal in an endowment fund was invested for a period of time at 6 percent, and inflation was running at 3 percent, the value of the principal at the end of the period, assuming the entire 6 percent earnings were expended, would be reduced 3 percent in real terms.

During the past 30 years, colleges became aware that, in order to execute their fiduciary duty, additional and commensurate risk would have to be taken to balance the equation; in other words, fiduciary duty requires the maintenance of purchasing power. This increased risk for incremental return was made by a change in the asset allocation percentages whereby a greater percentage was invested in the equity market. More recently, many institutions' investment committees have invested in real estate, venture capital, and oil and gas properties.

The primary responsibility of an investment committee is to set policy for the proper allocation of funds to various asset classes. In its simplest form, an investment committee could limit its asset classes to stocks, bonds, and cash and set an asset mix of 60 percent, 30 percent, and 10 percent, respectively. Further refinement would be to create additional asset classes for real estate and venture capital, as well as setting allocation percentages within major categories. In the case of stocks, suballocations could be created for international stocks, growth stocks, value stocks, etc. The proper monitoring of the allocation of funds to various asset classes and assurance that there is professional evaluation of the various money managers are the primary determinants of a successful investment policy.

The average asset allocation as of June 30, 1993, for 395 institutions responding to a national endowment survey was as follows:

Asset Class	Percent
Domestic common stocks	47.1%
Foreign currency common stocks	2.4%
Domestic fixed income	34.5%
Foreign currency fixed income	.8%
Cash and equivalents	10.1%
Equity real estate	2.2%
Other	2.9%
	100%

The primary investment management options available to the investment committee are to (1) buy and sell securities themselves, (2) use investment managers, (3) purchase shares in mutual funds, and (4) use any combination of the above. A CFO should direct the investment committee away from the first alternative unless the committee possesses the multiple skills required to carry out such transactions in a professional manner.

Spending Policy

The spending policy determines the amount of funds made available each year for student scholarships or for other endowment purposes. Historically, institutions set the spending limits to be equal to the amount of income earned in the form of interest and dividends. The amount was easy to determine and conveniently paralleled the common language in scholarship agreements restricting the amount available for spending to "income only."

The "income only" endowment restriction created a dilemma for investment committees. The need to generate a higher amount of cash yield required an asset allocation that was heavily weighted in fixed-income securities. Such a portfolio would have been expected to generate more cash than would a portfolio with a significant weighting in stocks. The dilemma arose from various studies that indicated stocks outperform bonds on a total return basis over time. Since 1926, the real return on stocks, bonds, and cash after the effect of inflation was 7 percent, 2 percent, and 0 percent, respectively. How could trustees carry out their fiduciary duty to maintain purchasing power of the endowment if the spending plan required a heavy weighting in fixed-income instruments?

To eliminate the problems created by the "income only" restriction in endowment agreements, and recognizing that it was directing endowment funds into asset classes that did not provide the best total return over time, legislation was passed in most states in the form of "The Management of Institutional Funds Act," which defined *income* more broadly and permitted a prudent amount of appreciation to be expended. The legislation permitted investment committees to search for the best possible total return, which includes income and appreciation, within a given level of risk without the internal restriction of generating a certain amount in the form of interest and dividends.

The new legislation permitted trustees to set endowment spending policies and investment policies that were not dependent on each other. The investment policy was not limited to fixed-income securities to satisfy the need of an aggressive spending policy, and the spending policy was not left unnecessarily low to compensate for a significant allocation to lower-yielding stocks. Committees should nevertheless be aware that a relationship does exist between the spending policy and the investment policy, and this relationship should be kept in mind when setting both policies.

Social Responsibility

Colleges have been pressured to further various societal goals by restricting investments in companies that do business in South Africa, in tobacco companies, in nuclear energy companies, and others. A recent book listed the following issues to consider when devising social investment criteria:

- Companies doing business in South Africa*
- Consumer rights and product quality
- Tobacco industry
- Alcoholic beverages industry
- Gambling industry
- Environmentalism
- Employee rights
- Racism
- Sexism
- Armaments, defense, and the military
- Animal rights
- Corporate philanthropy
- Northern Ireland
- Abortion
- Companies making and marketing infant formula
- Companies doing business with the People's Republic of China

Regardless of one's own views concerning past social issues associated with South Africa or any other current social issue, a college must examine the cost of social investing and relate it to the overall goal of providing an educational product at a reasonable price. The overall issue of just what constitutes social responsibility for a college or university takes on a different context when students are either dropping out or not applying initially because they can not afford the significant cost without further scholarship support.

The long-term effects on total return for most of the recently developed issues are not readily determinable; however, return losses from restricting investment in companies that do business in South Africa can be measured, as shown in Figure 10.1.

The margin of return between restricted and unrestricted portfolios has been reduced in the last few years because of the number of companies that have withdrawn from South Africa. Latest figures show that 90 percent of the companies in the S&P 500 qualify for SAF portfolios. As sanctions are lifted,

---

*Although South Africa is no longer a social issue, its financial history for investment serves as an example for social investments.

	One Year	Three Years	Five Years
S&P 500	30.6%	18.6%	15.4%
SAF S&P 500	30.1%	17.4%	14.0%
Reduced Return	.5%	1.2%	1.4%

ANNUALIZED RETURNS OF THE S&P 500 AND THE SOUTH AFRICA FREE (SAF) S&P 500 FOR ONE-, THREE-, AND FIVE-YEAR PERIODS ENDING DECEMBER 31, 1991

FIGURE 10.1

companies are reinvesting in South Africa and consequently will no longer qualify for inclusion in an SAF portfolio.

For example, non-U.S. investment in South Africa increased in 1991.[1] The number of non-U.S. companies with a direct investment in South Africa increased by 5 percent during 1991 from 433 companies in December 1990 to 454 companies in December 1991. As companies reestablish their business ties with South Africa, institutions with restrictions will again be holding portfolios with a distinct small capitalization bias and these stocks may not perform as well in the 1990s as they did in the 1980s.

As explained earlier, institutions need to balance the following equation: Total Return = Spending + Inflation. A reduction of one percentage point in total return for the cost of social investment criteria can only be offset by a reduction in endowment spending because inflation is a fixed number. *The lesson here is important. For every one percentage point reduction in total return, a college with a spending plan based on 5 percent of market value reduces the amount available for student scholarships or operations subsidy by 20 percent.*

An institution's governing board must ask itself if artificially restricting endowment returns for any of the aforementioned reasons is a practice of social responsibility or social irresponsibility. All of the issues may be meritorious, but trustees must consider them in conjunction with the overriding goal and mission of the university. Trustees should also be sensitive to the fact that the assets of the institution belong to the general public.

Colleges and universities exist to provide an educational product. Many parents and students can no longer afford a quality higher education, and most institutions are experiencing enrollment reductions partially due to inability to pay. A college or university's number-one mission is to provide a quality education at the lowest possible price. Artificially reducing endowment return, which has the effect of reducing endowment spending by 20 percent for every 1 percentage point reduction thwarts colleges and universities from carrying out that mission.

---

[1] "Foreigners Prefer Non-Equity Ties for Now," *South Africa Reporter* (December 1991), Investor Responsibility Research Center, 22.

There are ways to accomplish some of society's goals without detracting from a college's overall goal of providing a quality education at an affordable price. Colleges can do all of the following to promote the good intentions of the restrictions without reducing endowment return:

- Provide scholarships to students from South Africa
- Promote a smoke-free environment on campus
- Use recycled paper where appropriate and promote recycling of other commodities
- Promote responsible drinking

POOLED RESOURCES

The ideal investment program for an institution should be structured on a pooled basis. If an investment program is sound, it should be used for all endowments, both quasi-endowments and those endowments established by benefactors. The institution should discourage the establishment of endowments whose investment of funds is dictated by the benefactor. Such a policy also avoids the extraordinary administrative expense and responsibility for maintaining a variety of investment programs as opposed to a centralized pool of investments. Establishing a pooled program is primarily the responsibility of the chief financial officer and the officer responsible for soliciting endowments.

A pooled investment program dictates the need for a unitized accounting system for equitable distribution of principal and earnings to the individual endowments, both quasi- and benefactor-identified. Maintaining a unitized portfolio program is not difficult if certain basic information is available. This information includes the date and amount of each addition or withdrawal from a pooled investment fund and the market value of the fund at the time of each addition or withdrawal. The unit value at each month-end is used in calculating the new units added or the value of the units withdrawn during the subsequent month. Although some institutions calculate unit values quarterly or even less often, it should be realized that the resulting performance figures become less precise.

A successful investment program for an institution is a team arrangement between the chief financial officer, the chief executive officer, the investment committee, and, to a great extent, the officer responsible for soliciting endowment funds. Endowment giving to an institution can be encouraged by using the strategy with potential benefactors that if they give their money to your institution, as opposed to some other charitable opportunity, they will have an investment program that will allow for the growth of their principal base into a larger fund than what the other institution might be able to accomplish. It is also possible, as a marketing approach, to encourage those who have already given to strive for a larger endowment accumulation, which can be achieved not only through their giving but through the very successful investment program of the institution.

FOR FURTHER READING

Dunn, John A., Jr. "How Colleges Should Handle Their Endowment." *Planning for Higher Education* 19 (Spring 1991): 32–37.

Massy, William F. *Endowment: Perspectives, Policies, and Management.* Washington, DC: Association of Governing Boards of Universities and Colleges, 1990.

Silva, Paul V. *Unitizing Investment Pools.* Accounting Guidebook Series. Washington, DC: National Association of College and University Business Officers, 1993.

PART
V

·········

Major Expenditure
Areas

CHAPTER 11
••••••••

Administration

Administrative salary costs expanded during the past 20 years as a percentage of total institution costs. Colleges and universities attribute the explosion to, among other things, additional student services, increased government reporting requirements, special services for a diverse student body, intensified recruiting and aid demands, library and information technology support, and increased support to research.

This chapter is short because it is limited to addressing basic problems and providing an overview of the primary means for gaining productivity in administration. Each institution will develop its own program for addressing its many and varied administrative functions. The three primary techniques for addressing productivity in administration are reengineering (formerly business systems analysis), restructuring (formally reorganization), and outsourcing (formerly subcontracting). During the 1980s, American industry addressed manufacturing productivity problems with successful application of reengineering, restructuring, and outsourcing. It is now in the process of applying the same techniques to the administration sector.

At a CSC Exchange Forum for Senior Business and Information Systems Executives, held in Boston in 1992, the father of modern management science, Peter Drucker, admonished the assembled group for their failure to improve administration productivity over the past 30 years. He reminded them that untold billions of dollars had been invested in information technology, and productivity has remained flat.

Higher education will be asked to do much more with less and in the process achieve improved productivity and service.

REENGINEERING

Reengineering involves the overview of an administrative function or group of inter-related functions to outline required delivery of data, generation of reports, and common data availability. An overview is accompanied by a data plan analysis and required summary output. The systems analyst then designs a process flow that will produce the form of data, timing, and summary output. In the process of designing proper data generation, the computer will be used to maximum extent, and the use of administrators will be maintained at minimum staffing. In this manner, departments and reports are interrelated and reengineered—productivity is achieved. Employees are effectively used and the need for many other personnel can be eliminated by the efficient use of the computer. Peter Drucker is vindicated.

RESTRUCTURING

Many organizations are overstaffed and overdepartmentalized, requiring re-structuring consistent with the findings of reengineered processes. Restructuring should result in the following:

- Combination of departments with a common mission. Individual schools can share admissions, financial aid, and registration departments.
- Formal coordination of common services such as admissions, financial aid, registration, and bursar operations to improve customer delivery and efficiency.
- Reduction of middle management needs for multiple assistants, associates, and executive assistants.
- Elimination of contrived career path promotions and salary escalation.
- Formal accountability for performance expectations with commensurate financial adjustments. Conversely, replacement of weak producers.
- Broad sharing of secretaries in recognition that management personnel now perform traditional secretarial duties for typing, editing, and filing.

Restructuring concurrent with reengineering represents a bold change in higher education and will result in significant improvements in service delivery, productivity, and permanent cost reductions.

OUTSOURCING

Outsourcing is a matter of preparing a detailed specification of an in-house function and offering it as an RFP (request for proposal) to outside firms. Even if an outside firm is not selected to substitute for inside personnel, the very process can serve to tune up an in-house operation. Frequently, it is quite a shock to learn that an outside firm can provide better service at lower cost while realizing a profit. This is possible because the outside firm is a specialist with a large base of similar businesses. Also, the outside firm has probably already reengineered and restructured its operation.

Outsourcing can also be a means of removing a unionized function. Although it is true that the outside firm may have a union, its problems will not be your problems. If you decide to reduce personnel, you call the contractor and work out a reduction in force. If the union people strike and disrupt operations, you terminate the contract and sign on with a competitor.

The combination of reengineering, restructuring, and selected outsourcing will make it possible to significantly improve administrative productivity. Systems engineering will finally find a place in the sun.

CHAPTER 12

Academics and Faculty

t is now time for the business officer (me!) to write the chapter on academics and faculty. In a people-intensive business, the faculty and the administrators who directly support faculty represent the largest concentration of expenditures in higher education. Academics represents the production of higher education, and if costs are to be contained, this area has to be addressed and changes have to be made.

Respected members of the faculty can succinctly define management in the academic area. A faculty senate president referred to the management of faculty as being analogous to "herding cats." The provost of a large university described the task as "the untrained attempting to lead the ungovernable." A landmark book on college leadership refers to the process as "organized anarchy." I think any executive in a position of management responsibility for higher education would find these statements descriptive of the challenge.

Academics is not only the most difficult area in higher education to manage but presents the most complicated number of cost variables that can influence quality and productivity.[1] Many expressions have been suggested in the hope of avoiding the problems associated with a common business term for results, but none of them is as correct as the word *productivity*. Webster's and Roget's descriptions conjure all the proper terminology for productivity including "results, quality, benefits, abundance, creativity, fertility, yields, devotion, profit, and net return on wealth." All of these apply, in some part, to the instructional process in the industry of higher education.

---

[1]Nathaniel H. Karol and Sigmund G. Ginsburg, *Managing the Higher Education Enterprise* (New York: John Wiley and Sons, 1980), 152.

This chapter considers many means of improving productivity to achieve containment of cost for the instructional function of an institution and the generation of a positive bottom line: "Yes, Virginia, there is a bottom line in academics." The bottom line in academics is the margin that can be generated at the classroom level on a per seat basis achieved while producing a quality graduate. In industry, margin is the accomplishment of a business mission, measured by deducting the many expenditures required to achieve an end result from the corresponding revenue generated. A similar situation exists in academics. Margin at the instruction level is measured by deducting the many expenditures to support a student in a classroom seat from the net tuition revenue generated by the student. The product is different—a well-educated graduate—but the necessary end result of a competitive and financially viable business is the same.

THE REASONS FOR HIGH ACADEMIC AND FACULTY COSTS

During the past 30 years, there have been many changes in academics resulting in a situation where the cost of educating a student escalated at an impressive rate. Fortunately for higher education, institutions were able to pass on these costs to the students by increasing tuition rates at an equally impressive rate. The ability to increase revenue in proportion to rising costs protected the margin generated per seat and postponed for the industry of higher education an impending day of reckoning. Cost must be stabilized in order to stabilize tuition rates and once again make higher education afford- able and accessible. If costs are not contained, institutions will incur deficits and lose financial viability.

On the premise that significant tuition increases will no longer be possible, this chapter is devoted to identifying cost containment opportunities based on an understanding of the many changes that have contributed to substantial per seat cost escalation over the past 30 years. Changes in the instruction process that have resulted in high costs include the following:

- *Widespread adoption of tenure programs.* Tenure gained a foothold in the United States in the 1920s. Today approximately 94 percent of the faculty in the United States are associated with institutions that have a tenure program. The primary exception to tenure programs are the two-year community colleges, which mostly employ instruc- tors on a contract basis.[2] Productivity problems associated with tenure are numerous and reviewed later in this chapter.

---

[2]Kenneth P. Mortimer, Maigue Bagshaw, and Andrew T. Masland, *Flexibility in Academic Staffing: Effective Policies and Practices,* ASHE-ERIC Higher Education Report no. 1 (Washing- ton, DC: Association for the Study of Higher Education, 1985), 15.

- *Increased percentage of faculty with PhDs.* Many institutions seeking prestige and recognition by accrediting agencies have directed that a greater percentage of PhD faculty be used in the classrooms, instead of masters-level instructors. Higher credentials demand higher salaries.
- *Teacher/scholar base salary higher than that of teacher.* Faculty members who are expected to conduct research and write, in addition to teach, command a higher salary than professors who only teach.[3]
- *Base teaching load reductions.* The faculty, accrediting agencies, and state associations have lobbied continuously, with great success, for reduced teaching loads.
- *Class size reductions.* In addition to reduced teaching loads, the faculty, supported by students, has lobbied for smaller classes to enhance teaching quality. The combination of reduced teaching load and smaller classes provides a significant reduction in the number of students attended by each faculty member.
- *Teaching overload elimination.* In the past, many professors taught during the summer for a stipend, which was less per course than the course proportion of their base salary. Summer teaching is now accomplished by hiring additional faculty.
- *Reduced salary subsidy and reduced teaching load associated with trend from endowed to named professorships.* Endowed professorships are usually funded in full for total salary, while many named professorships are partially endowed with the balance of base salary absorbed in current operations. The trend in recent years has shifted from endowed professorships to more institution-subsidized named professorships. Further, faculty occupying named professorship positions commonly do not teach more than one section a semester, if that.
- *Additional faculty to support reduced teaching load.* Teaching load reductions, reduced class size, elimination of teaching overload, reduced use of adjuncts, and decreasing support from endowments for professorships require the hiring of additional full-time faculty to make up the difference in section loading.[4]
- *Institution-funded summer stipends for scholarly pursuits.* In those disciplines where there is a shortage of PhDs, faculty are demanding a guaranteed summer stipend in addition to a market base salary.
- *Increased institution-research funding.* Some faculty members are unsuccessful in writing proposals to solicit third-party research funding

---

[3] Thomas W. Longfitt, "The Costs of Higher Education: Lessons to Learn from the Health Care Industry," *Change* (November/December 1990), 14.

[4] James M. Shuart, "One View of the Near Future in Higher Education," KMPG Peat Marwick, *Management Issues for Colleges and Universities,* July 1989, 3.

from foundations, industry, or individuals. As a result, there has been increasing demand for institution-financed research. (Could the problem be, in certain cases, that sponsors are not interested in funding proposals because the requests are not appropriate to society's needs?)

- *Increased sponsored research with progressively less indirect cost recovery.* The government is resisting indirect cost recovery on contracts. It is disallowing certain expenses, many for good reasons, and, in some cases, limiting the percentage of recovery.

- *Increased support personnel services and facilities for larger faculty.* The increased number of faculty relative to the number of students has created a larger organization requiring more direct administrative support for space and services.

- *Increased number of graduate assistants.* More graduate students have been granted institution-funded financial aid in the form of graduate assistantships to support the expanded faculty in their research and teaching responsibilities.[5]

- *Larger libraries required to support research and scholarly pursuits.* As education became more complicated and more faculty members were hired as a result of reduced teaching loads, libraries were expanded to support demand.[6] In addition, computer-assisted research support has expanded.

- *Pressure for increased percentage of tenured positions.* Most faculty members covet tenure, and there is continuous pressure on institutions to increase the percentage of faculty positions that are tenured or on a tenure track.

- *CPI plus salary demands.* National academic organizations maintain detailed records on salary trends for faculty members, as does the popular *Chronicle of Higher Education.* This database has enabled faculty in recent years to, in effect, ratchet salary levels and play catch-up on perceived losses in purchasing power.

- *Relief from nonacademic counseling responsibility for students.* Thirty years ago, the faculty provided a certain amount of counseling and, in many cases, lived in residences with the students. The faculty will no longer accept these responsibilities, and this has given great impetus to the development of comprehensive and expensive student affairs divisions.[7]

---

[5]Joseph Froomkin, *The Crisis in Higher Education* (Montpelier, VT: The Academy of Political Science, 1983), 100-01.

[6]Howard R. Bowen, *The Costs of Higher Education* (San Francisco: Jossey-Bass, Inc., 1980), 66.

[7]Alan Deutschman, "Why Universities Are Shrinking," *Fortune* (24 September 1990): 108.

PROBLEMS WITH TENURE

As can be seen, so many factors have contributed to a drop in productivity in the area of instruction over the past 30 years. Thus, cost-conscious higher education officials will look toward ways of developing a program for the management of instruction costs that could restore affordable education beyond K-12.

While reviewing faculty productivity problems, the issue of faculty/student ratios should be addressed. For many years published ratios have been presented as a means of judging the academic quality of an institution. The public has been led to believe that an institution with a low ratio is academically better than an institution with a higher ratio. Unfortunately, the ratios are determined by taking total full-time equivalent students and dividing by the total full-time equivalent faculty. This produces a misleading conclusion when one understands that a large number of faculty members, particularly in research institutions, are devoting most, if not all their time to internal or third-party funded research. A low faculty/student ratio is not indicative of faculty productivity in the classroom. The ratios as currently calculated should be discontinued for the purpose of making comparisons between institutions.

Fundamental to improving productivity of the instructional process is a discussion of tenure. Tenure is a many splendored thing for faculty members who are so vested. How could any individual deny that a lifetime of independence and security coupled with a comfortable livelihood is not the best of all worlds? The favorable and unfavorable features of tenure have been reviewed endlessly, and this book will not extend that debate. Tenure is enjoyed by many faculty, judges, attorneys, and, in recent years, a growing body of public employees (albeit de facto). During an era of growth and economic strength the government and higher education could afford the luxury of unlimited tenure because productivity demands were limited in a non-competitive cost plus environment. Our country is now faced with international competition, and our institutions of higher education are faced with national competition; higher education may also face international competition later in the decade. It is time to take a hard look at tenure and what role it will play in a highly competitive marketplace during the remainder of the 1990s.

Competition is the impetus for improved productivity in any human endeavor. Productivity includes competitive wages, the application of capital to reduce labor applied, quality, quantity, creative change, and inspiration. Certainly, higher education, in order to provide an affordable education, desires a faculty body that is hardworking, current in one's field, able to motivate students, creative in the use of the latest capital equipment applications (particularly electronics), willing to be responsible for as many students as is comfortable and equitable, proud of their profession, and more than happy to provide time to students who are in academic difficulty. This set of conditions constitutes a productive, satisfying opportunity for a professional educator.

Tenure introduces the following productivity problems, particularly if an organization is stable or is in a downsizing mode, as are many institutions of higher education at this time:

- Independence can be a problem, because tenured faculty members may pursue whatever research they are interested in, regardless of whether it is in the best interest of the student, the institution, or society.[8]

- Security can be a problem because the faculty member is not subject to competition from other faculty members internally or externally.

- Freedom must be a problem, because if it weren't it wouldn't take so long for constructive change or cooperation between the various disciplines to result.[9]

- There has been a slowness to adopt new pedagogical techniques that would greatly enhance education, such as computers, electronic databases, and voice, video, and database integration.[10]

- Tenure created an additional complication for higher education when the government decided to eliminate mandatory retirement and allow high-priced senior faculty, whose productivity may be declining, to work indefinitely.

- Those who have tenure have great freedom to say whatever they want, to whomever they want. Conversely, those who are attempting to "earn" tenure have to be extremely careful in their personal and professional actions. This situation does not provide a creative, spontaneous environment for positive direction and development of the most important industry in the country.

- In a period of downsizing at a college, (1) there is no room to bring in young, new PhDs, the best of whom would demand tenure track; and (2) the mix of faculty between tenured, tenure track, nontenure track, and adjunct will fall out of balance, increasing classroom seat costs. This will occur because higher paid tenured and tenure track

---

[8]Howard R. Bowen, *The Costs of Higher Education* (San Francisco: Jossey-Bass, Inc., 1990), 66-67.

[9]Charles J. Sykes, *ProfScam: Professors and the Demise of Higher Education* (New York: St. Martin's Press, 1988), 11-12.

[10]Murray Turoff, *Online Education: Perspectives on a New Environment*, ed., Linda M. Harasim (New York: Praeger Publishers, 1990), xi-xxi.

faculty will be retained and the lower paid nontenure track and adjunct faculty will be laid off.[11]

- Course loads shift by academic discipline from year to year. A fixed body of tenured faculty makes it impossible to fine-tune course loading between disciplines and protect seat costs. The problem is further complicated by the industry's reluctance to extend the number of years delay for tenure consideration to slow down the buildup of fixed-cost tenure appointments.
- In a declining market, many of the most productive faculty on staff are rejected for tenured appointments and must leave the institution after the tenure "gestation" period.

COST CONTAINMENT RECOMMENDATIONS
Review the Tenure Program

Cost containment recommendations for an institution with a tenure program include short-term and long-term features. For the short term, periodically offer a tenure buyout to senior faculty, to be decided upon within a window of time. This will reduce the number of tenured positions, provide balance in the faculty structure, and maintain opportunities for young PhDs to enter the organization. The long-term recommendation is to phase out an institution's tenure program and replace it with a renewable multiyear contract program.

Review Class Size and Faculty Loading

The second major problem for regaining productivity is the dwindling number of students that each faculty member is responsible for teaching. This situation results from the reduced number of sections taught by a faculty member and the reduced number of students in each class. It is interesting to note that teaching at all levels in the United States is totally out of balance with what is needed. At the K-12 education level, class sizes are being increased for students of an age requiring individualized instruction, while at the higher education level, where qualified students should require significantly less individualized instruction, there is pressure to reduce class size.

A recommended improvement for increasing the student/faculty ratio is to establish teaching load standards, relative to sponsored scholarly activities; that is, establish a teaching load standard of three sections per semester to be adjusted downward only for scholarly activity sponsored by third-party funding. In effect, a faculty member can buy out one-third or more of the course load assignment by bringing in research funds equal to the course load reduction. For example, when a tenured or tenure track faculty member

---

[11]Andrew Hacker, "Too Many Full Professors: A Top-Heavy Pyramid," *The Chronicle of Higher Education* (4 March 1992): B1-B2.

makes $60,000 a year and teaches three sections per semester, each section costs $10,000. In this example, the faculty member's teaching load could be reduced to two sections in a given semester with the institution being reimbursed $10,000 through a research project for the third section. The purpose of establishing a standard teaching load is to provide equity for the institution and avoid instances where aggressive faculty members are able to talk their department chairs into unrealistic load reductions.

A second recommendation is that class size be continually monitored. This will entail establishing class size range standards and canceling sections if registrations fall below a given level. It should be recognized that there are practical differences regarding class size by subject. For example, a freshman English composition course should have a smaller class size because of the attention required for correction of papers. In contrast, an introductory accounting course is dependent primarily on a textbook with examples, and class time is primarily devoted to lecture; thus a larger section size would be practical. Considerable leverage in increasing the average section size for an institution can be achieved through large lecture sections requiring mainly audio/visual communication. What a perfect application for TV monitors and satellite linkage![12] Better yet, in certain instances, why not have the students remain at home or in their residence halls; activate voice, video, and data linkage online to the lecture halls; and save classroom/facility cost. In addition, the students could record the lectures on a VCR and review the tapes before an exam.

Review Research Practices

A third area of difficulty in maintaining productivity is research work in general. Work performed on research that is not fully paid for by a third party will be passed along to the students through tuition increases. Research is, therefore, an area of productivity that inadvertently raises the costs for instruction, both direct and indirect.

First, let us look at direct costs. To be competitive, a research proposal must be responsive to the specifications and must be price sensitive. Therefore, if a faculty member, such as in the earlier example, is making $10,000 per section taught and prepares a proposal for a grant to buy release time, his or her time in the classroom may be covered by an adjunct who earns perhaps only $3,000 for teaching that section. The proposal in this situation will, therefore, possibly list $3,000 for direct costs rather than the $10,000 for the salary of the individual faculty member who will work on the project. This would be a splendid approach if there was only intermittent activity in the research sector and the sum of all research was not an appreciable portion of the institution's

---

[12]Charles E. Feasley, *Serving Learners at a Distance: A Guide to Program Practices*, ASHE-ERIC Higher Education Research Report no. 5 (Washington, DC: Association for the Study of Higher Education, 1983), 1.

business. However, what may happen is that research business in the institution grows, and the balance within the classroom between tenured, tenured track, nontenured track, and adjunct faculty is disturbed by the mounting support for sponsored research. Consequently, more tenured and tenure track faculty are hired to satisfy research demands and maintain faculty mix. The end result is that the institution does not recover appropriate direct costs because tenured faculty are working on the research, their replacements in the classroom are high-priced tenured faculty, and recovery from research sponsors is at the adjunct salary level. The difference is made up by increasing tuition to recover the portion of direct cost not paid by grants.

Another problem with research is indirect cost recovery. It seems that everyone, including the administration in higher education, has difficulty understanding why an organization that sponsors research should have to pay for indirect costs when most indirect costs are currently paid for by the institution. Like any business arrangement, an institution working on a research project should be reimbursed for the time a faculty member spends on a project, fringe benefits, project expenses (e.g., computer time, grad assistants, secretaries, supplies, travel), and an overhead rate that recognizes all institutional support costs. In addition, research requires space, equipment, insurance, security, and financial administration. As mentioned earlier, recovery of costs might not be material if there is only intermittent research activity and it is not an appreciable part of the total institution's business. However, if research was half the business and instruction was the other half, then certainly roughly half of all the indirect overhead costs of the institution should be borne by organizations sponsoring research. The government is reluctant to pay full indirect costs as negotiated, while foundations and industry are reluctant to pay anything. The end result is insufficient recovery of indirect costs and the need to finance these expenditures through tuition.

More recently, government investigations have disclosed that some costs included in the overhead pools of certain large research institutions are for unnecessary expenditures that not only have nothing to do with research but actually are not necessary to the administration of the institution. In this situation, the government is right in not reimbursing the institution, and taxpayers, students, and their parents should object as well. Unfortunately, the government is overreacting to questionable practices by certain institutions, not only rejecting legitimate overhead expenditures but attempting to place arbitrary caps on negotiated rates.[13]

---

[13]Bureau of National Affairs, *Federal Contracts Report*, 15 July 1991.

Improve Long-Term Strategic Planning

The fourth major area of productivity problems is the lack of long-term strategic planning in higher education. It will be impossible to prevent per seat cost from going totally out of control within a downsize condition unless there is long-term planning for the direction of the institution and anticipated section loading on individual academic departments. To contain the relative seat cost, it will be necessary to maintain a balance between tenured, tenure track, nontenure track, and rank loading by department. There is a declining salary/section cost, for faculty within the four labor categories, with professor being the most expensive and adjunct being the least expensive. If these instruction rankings get out of balance through reduction of the lower-cost faculty, the per seat cost will increase exponentially at a time when cost containment is of paramount importance. Strategic planning will allow the deans and the provost to use attrition, tenure buyouts, controlled research activity, and selected reductions in force to achieve balanced section loading by discipline.

Consider Strategic Alliances with Other Institutions

Although there is little research on the subject that would support projected savings, there should be many opportunities to develop strategic alliances with neighboring institutions that would streamline operations. These alliances are analogous to the sharing of major diagnostic and treatment equipment among hospitals within the medical industry.

Strategic alliances allow institutions to broaden academic offerings by picking up courses from other institutions that are not available within their own institution, as well as providing institutions the opportunity to eliminate certain sections that are not productive because of inadequate enrollment levels.[14] It is possible that these types of alliances could also open up additional degree programs if packaged properly. For instance, a business school could develop a master's level program in manufacturing operations if it were to team up with a local institution that could provide the appropriate engineering courses to fill out the curriculum.

Joint ventures provide revenue enhancement by offering new programs or by improving market penetration and cutting costs in existing programs. It is difficult to beat the combination of added revenues and reduced costs in any market situation. But, in a downsizing environment, the combination might

---

[14]Deutschman, "Why Universities Are Shrinking," *Fortune* (24 September 1990): 106.

mean survival. The evaluation of a strategic alliance should be supported by an analysis of an institution's current programs. A proper analysis requires the use of a cost system that will identify per seat net revenue versus cost of all disciplines and all course offerings. The results of this analysis will reveal that certain sections or disciplines are losing money at a rate that begs review to determine whether they should be continued as loss leaders, farmed out to another institution, or dropped completely. If a course does not serve a strategic purpose, then dropping a course, or even a discipline, and eliminating a margin drain is the proper decision.

The ultimate use of a per seat net revenue versus cost system is the evaluation of margin generated by disciplines, schools, colleges, and the university as a whole. Margin at the instruction level is what should support the education industry.

Implement a Salary Administration Program

Industry developed salary administration programs many decades ago. Most institutions of higher education have now developed salary administration programs for their administrators, but few, if any, have implemented a similar program for faculty members.

Salary administration in its simplest form is the establishment of salary ranges for positions of commensurate responsibilities. It is understood that personnel hired within a given classification come into the grade range according to their ability, performance, and experience. The midpoint in the salary grade for a position is usually about where the market is for the average person successfully performing the requirements of the position. Salary ranges should be adjusted annually to reflect some part of the market's inflationary impact on the ranges granted for each position.

Determining supply and demand for positions within the marketplace has always been a problem for salary administration programs. A particular position might be similar to a different position within the organization regarding degree of education, difficulty, responsibility, and impact on the organization as a whole if the responsibilities are poorly performed. Frequently, supply and demand in the marketplace will run up the salary demands for a particular position far beyond what is determined through analysis to be reasonable. However, that is the marketplace, and if one is going to hire talented people one must pay the rates demanded. Unfortunately, demands change, and salary administrators are reluctant to change pay grades for what might be an ephemeral situation and risk throwing the system out of balance. It is not the purpose of this book to try to solve that problem, only to recognize that marketplace supply and demand exist, particularly in the faculty area where industry demands for students in certain fields frequently create growth in such areas as engineering and business.

In spite of these problems, a salary administration program can be developed for faculty that will provide balance, equity, and cost containment features similar to those achieved in administrative areas. A well-maintained salary administration program should be coupled with salary rewards based on merit and performance. Performance evaluations should be in writing, presented in person, and signed by both parties in order to ensure proper communication. In addition, proper documentation is invaluable during organization reductions.

Be Wary of Unions

Having discussed basing financial rewards on performance, we can move on to a review of union representation and its effect on productivity. Unions in general do not foster quality performance, and they certainly do not provide for the development of the brightest and best in any organization. Most unions support the concept that they are representing the entire work force, and therefore, whatever gains they can negotiate should be granted equally to all personnel within the represented organization. Institutions of higher education with personnel represented by unions, whether they be administrators or faculty, are going to find themselves at a great disadvantage in the highly competitive marketplace of the 1990s. The brightest and best will not be rewarded or encouraged to compete in the market, restructuring of organization or curriculum will be difficult, and salary pressures will be unrelated to business circumstances.

Use Graduate Assistant Programs

Another opportunity for cost containment is to use graduate assistant programs. Graduate assistants are graduate-level students who are working within academia to earn tuition forgiveness or stipends to fulfill financial obligations for their education. The manner in which they are now used, either as instructors or administrators, creates a financial problem. Their hourly pay rate is approximately equal to that of an entry-level undergraduate student in the industrial marketplace. They are expected to perform services for the faculty that for the most part are understood to be related to teaching or research work. Frequently, the work they perform is below their academic and intellectual capabilities, and there may not be enough work to keep them productively busy. Another concern is their use as instructors, which may shortchange undergraduate students who are entitled to the teaching talents of a terminally degreed professional classroom teacher. Also, paying a professor to teach and then substituting a graduate assistant for the professor is a duplication of institutional expenditure. Finally, if certain sections can be taught by graduate assistants, it follows that the institution should retain fewer professors and hire more lower-paid master-level instructors.

Graduate assistant programs should be reviewed carefully to make sure that work performed is worthy of salary paid and contributes to the mission of the institution. If administrative assignments are not at a professional level, then the work should be performed by a secretary or a clerk to reduce cost. If an inordinate number of teaching assignments are passed on to graduate assistants, the institution should change its mix of professors and instructors to reduce cost. However, the institution must maintain selected assignments of graduate assistants to teaching in order to fulfill the requirement for training PhDs.

Trends in Faculty and Per-Seat Costs

The following two figures dramatize what has happened during the past 30 years to faculty costs and the impact on per-seat cost in the classroom. Figure 12.1 provides a hypothetical example, in constant dollars, to show the cost implication of just three major variables on cost per seat in a section. The first variable is a drop in sections taught per year from eight to five, which may be configured as three one semester and two the following semester. The second variable is a drop in the number of students in a section from 30 to 20, and the third variable is the increase in the average salary of the professor from $48,000 to $70,000, based on collective salary ratcheting in constant dollars. The impact of these three variables on cost per seat is dramatic: Annual cost per seat increases from $200 to $700, a more than threefold increase.

Figure 12.2 presents a whimsical vision of what might happen to our industry if higher education resources are not managed. Since the beginning of the demographic decline of 18-year-olds, which started in 1979, revenues stayed in balance with expenditures as higher education increased tuition

Arrangement	Previous Instruction Arrangement	Current Instruction Arrangement
Number of Sections Per Year	8	5
Avg. Number of Students in Section	30	20
Number of Students Taught in Year	240	100
(No Sections × Avg. Class Size)		
Annual Salary of Professor	$48,000	$70,000
ANNUAL COST PER SEAT		
(Annual Salary of Professor ÷ Number of		
Students Taught in Year)	$ 200	$ 700

IMPACT OF REDUCED TEACHING LOAD, REDUCED SECTION SIZE, AND TEACHER/SCHOLAR SALARY ON ANNUAL COST PER SEAT (IN CONSTANT DOLLARS)

FIGURE 12.1

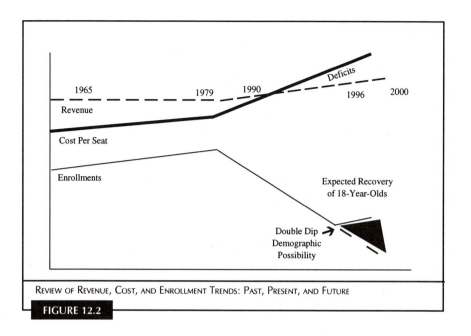

REVIEW OF REVENUE, COST, AND ENROLLMENT TRENDS: PAST, PRESENT, AND FUTURE

FIGURE 12.2

rates at double-digit levels to absorb uncontrolled spending. By 1990, absorbing costs became difficult with decreased enrollments and margins beginning to diminish. Going into the 1990s, many institutions incurred deficits as enrollments continued to decline, costs for the most part remained unchecked, and discounting of tuition for financial aid became unbearable. The shaded area at the bottom of the chart portends what was discussed earlier in this book as a possible second demographic problem if costs are not contained and spiraling tuition rates not controlled. Although there will be a slight increase in the number of 18-year-olds available to pursue higher education after 1996, there will be a body of them who normally would have pursued an education but find the net price of tuition prohibitive. A self-inflicted second demographic problem would be unfortunate during any era, but it would be a tragedy with the United States entering a highly competitive international marketplace.

Take Advantage of Data Communications

Finally, faculty productivity can be improved through the use and application of data communications. Here's how:

1. Accelerate the education process and improve interest in complicated subject matter by using the computer to rapidly present concepts. Examples: Enter an accounting journal entry and allow the student to see

on the monitor its impact on the profit-and-loss statement, balance sheet, and cash flow; have the student listen to the spoken foreign language pronunciation as he or she reads; have mathematical equations move across an electronic chalkboard; access word definitions and synonyms on-screen with a click; demonstrate concurrent historical events on a map flowing across an electronic screen.

2. Provide all classrooms and resident rooms with voice, fax, video, and data link capability. Link the same building sites to a satellite dish.

   • Select the best lectures on a given subject and transmit them to selected rooms and locations. Allow students to copy the lectures on their VCR for playback at a convenient time or to review before an exam.

   • If students are not available for a class, allow them to "attend" class through their voice, video, and data hookup in their residence building, home if they are a commuter via modem, or satellite if they are out of town (maybe after the year 2000).

   • Charge a nominal tuition of students who wish to audit a course through voice, video, and data that does not require the use of a seat in the classroom.

   • Offer a curriculum for which it is not cost-effective to build a full-service faculty by supplementing required sections with voice, video, and data connections with other institutions.

   • Conduct education throughout the world via satellite voice-fax-video-data linkage, and the Internet. The opportunities to make the faculty more productive through creative applications are unlimited.

WHAT THE FUTURE HOLDS

Four points summarize the importance of this chapter.

1. Dedicated faculty members are probably the most important professional group in our country at this time. In order for the United States to remain competitive, it will be necessary that the brightest, best, and most education-minded individuals be attracted to the teaching profession and that they be handsomely rewarded for quality performance and productivity. The demand for talented faculty in combination with the terminal-degree level of education should entitle them to command salaries equitable with the two terminally degreed professions of medicine and law, after a 25 percent adjustment for summer release. (If higher education should decide to operate their institutions 12 months a year to improve productivity, the faculty would certainly be entitled to salaries equal to those of the other terminally degreed professions.)

2. The faculty must recognize that the student is higher education's primary customer. It should be understood that this does not mean offering "grade inflation," as has occurred in recent years. Rather, it means respect, response, and relevancy.

3. It is possible that the expected faculty shortage, particularly in the technical fields, may be avoided if section loading, class size, and faculty mix are properly managed. This possibility is strengthened by a shrinking body of students in the near future and a slower growth pattern into the next century. Teaching and scholarship activity in support of relevant research is a rewarding profession and young people should be encouraged and supported to pursue the PhD. Handsome salaries for productive faculty will help to attract more young people to the profession.

4. Although faculty will be reluctant to rally around the flag when it comes to containment of cost per seat in the classroom, it will be a necessity if higher education is to remain affordable to those young people who want access.

CHAPTER 13

The Physical Plant

T he physical plant of an institution is the land, buildings, playing fields, roads, parking lots, and all the electrical, mechanical, and plumbing support required to service the people who occupy the facilities. Although higher education is a labor-intensive business, the second largest cost of running an institution is the acquisition, construction, and upkeep of the physical plant. The facilities are used to house professional people, and in the case of research institutions very expensive facilities are required. The physical plant is home to employees eight or more hours a day and to resident students 24 hours a day. Facilities should create an attractive environment, be maintained, and in most cases include amenities like air-conditioning. An attractive facility is also of immense importance for marketing the institution and retaining all constituencies.

The major types of buildings on the campus support classroom instruction and laboratories, student housing, and administration. This chapter will review the planning required to maintain a cost-effective physical plant and the management systems required for support. Maintaining appropriate financial support for the physical plant is frustrating because expenditures can be postponed during an extended period of financial difficulty.[1] In the past 20 years, many institutions have adopted a program of deferred maintenance, usually unwittingly and on an unplanned basis. Serious deferred maintenance commenced in 1979 when double-digit inflation gripped the country, creating financial difficulties for everyone, particularly for higher education because its

---

[1]Howard R. Bowen, *The Costs of Higher Education: How Much Do Colleges and Universities Spend Per Student and How Much Should They Spend?* (San Francisco: Jossey-Bass, Inc., 1980), 210.

primary costs—personnel—were inflation paced. Every effort was made to keep payroll in step with inflation, at the expense of the physical plant. College administrators did what they had to do to maintain a viable institution: They diverted funds to salaries, resulting in a national higher education accumulation of approximately $75 billion in deferred maintenance, $25 billion of which administrators judge to require immediate attention. Unfortunately, deferred maintenance is cumulative and unless addressed will overwhelm many institutions.

Another phenomenon that has occurred during the past 15 years is families embracing higher education as a total life experience. This resulted in an extraordinary demand for on-campus housing. Although construction for academic and administrative requirements leveled off as a result of declining demographics, the demand for housing and new construction increased. Institutions had to respond to the housing demand to maintain market position. If the consumer wanted room and board, the institution that did not respond was at a distinct market disadvantage. However, it is important to mention that smart management supplemented on-campus construction with off-campus leased facilities to accommodate later capacity reduction.

The unfortunate part of the demand for housing during this period, particularly in the private sector, was that institutions either spent operating funds for construction or incurred additional debt, with the commensurate mortgage/ maintenance cycle creating yet another pressure on tuition rates. However, cash flow resulting from board and room activity as an auxiliary enterprise created a great potential for margin because of the relatively fixed cost. If American families continue to demand on-campus room and board, higher education will have a permanent source of margin in the auxiliary business sector of room and board. If management is attuned to the situation, it will be able to use the revenue excesses realized on room and board to reduce campuswide deferred maintenance in a planned fashion.

One way to help avoid the problem of deferred maintenance is to create a physical plant restoration and replacement funded reserve.

RESTORATION AND REPLACEMENT OF PHYSICAL PLANT

A restoration and replacement reserve is of particular importance to not-for-profit business because most institutions do not "fund" their depreciation and, therefore, do not have an opportunity to build up a cash reserve for eventual replacement of the facilities. Because a not-for-profit organization is not subject to income taxes, it is not motivated to take depreciation as an expense. In addition, fund accounting does not lend itself to the traditional profit-and-loss approach to monitor current operations.

A feature of higher education that lends itself to a restoration and replacement concept is the fact that, for the most part, its physical plant, if properly maintained, does not become obsolete. Classrooms and offices are traditional, and housing requirements have not changed in any major sense over the past 100 years. Therefore, if the physical plant is maintained in its original condition in perpetuity, there should be no reason to tear it down in 30 or 50 years; thus depreciation of that asset, whether at original or market cost, really does not make any sense. What does make sense is (1) establishment of a reserve fund that will, on a scheduled basis, maintain the facilities and all support systems in their original condition; and (2) maintenance of a stable annual fund transfer from current operations to the reserve within the plant fund, increasing only for inflation and the addition of new structures to the program.

In 1979, I developed a physical plant maintenance program for the purpose of avoiding deferred maintenance and unscheduled extraordinary demands on current operations. Highlights of that program follow.

PHYSICAL PLANT RESTORATION AND REPLACEMENT STUDY

Purpose

- To establish a technique for planning long-range expenditures for the restoration and replacement of the college's physical assets
- To anticipate the timing of restoration and replacement decisions in order to (1) reduce maintenance cost to the college and (2) maintain the aesthetic appearance of the campus
- To recognize that long-range restoration and replacement expenditures should be incrementally provided for as a current funding requirement each year

Definition

Restoration or replacement is the ultimate maintenance decision that has to be made concerning existing physical assets. The timing of the expenditures can be influenced by (1) the prohibitive cost of continued corrective maintenance, (2) the aesthetic deterioration of the asset, (3) the safety needs of personnel, or (4) the obsolescence of the asset due either to technological change or contemporary taste. The decision to proceed with a restoration or replacement expenditure is influenced by the availability of the large sums of money required for this type of maintenance.

Expenditures for restoration and replacement are usually not specifically provided for in institutional long-term fiscal planning. However, the maintenance expenditures that precede a restoration or replacement expenditure are provided for through the year-to-year operating budgets for preventive and corrective maintenance.

Expenditures Considered in Analysis

The expenditures included in the analysis were defined as individual projects in excess of $10,000 that are not included in the annual operating budget.

The approach to accumulating information for the study was a physical inventory of buildings, their internal and external systems, and outside grounds structures. The assets were then reduced to convenient costing factors such as square footage of walls, roofs, asphalt areas, etc., and, in the mechanical and electrical areas, number of units and footage. All projected expenditures were based on current cost. Life expectancy for individual projects was determined in order to time-phase expenditures.

Figure 13.1 contains a list of major items considered in the analysis.

Buildings			
Exterior		*Interior*	
Walls	Roofs	Floors/stairs	Electrical systems
Stairs	Doors	Walls	Mechanical systems
Porches	Windows	Ceilings	Plumbing systems
Grounds			
Electrical systems	Roads	Tennis courts	
Water systems	Parking lots	Playing fields	

MAJOR ITEMS CONSIDERED IN THE EXPENDITURES ANALYSIS

FIGURE 13.1

Certain items such as furniture and floor covering were segregated as either an operating expense or a restoration or replacement item. Furniture in the resident and classroom buildings was considered a major replacement because of hard usage and relatively uniform deterioration on a building-by-building basis. Furniture in all other areas was considered as random replacement and therefore included in the operating budgets. Floor covering on large open areas was considered major and included in the analysis.

Assumptions Used in Study

- The study covered 40 years, which was the expected time lapse before the slate roofs and exterior brick walls on the earliest buildings would require attention.
- Projects with a life expectancy of 20 years or less were repeated in the study, that is, 20-year projects entered twice, 10-year projects entered four times, etc.

- The smaller buildings on campus were not included in the study because individual projects for them would be less than $10,000. The restoration and replacement funds required for small buildings were included in the operating budgets.
- Expenditures were totaled and a cumulative inflation factor applied by year.
- Average income earned on the reserve balance from investments was calculated and applied to the average reserve balance for each year.
- The study was updated every three years to review reserve activity and add new physical plant structures.

Examples of the Maintenance Life Cycle for Assets Included in the Program

Slate Roof

- *Preventive maintenance:* Periodic visual review to note loose, cracked, or missing slates.
- *Corrective maintenance:* Replacement of individual slates or sections of slates.
- *Charge to restoration and replacement reserve:* Removal of all slates on a building, repair of roof paneling as required, and remounting or replacement of slate.

Parking Lot

- *Preventive maintenance:* Visual inspection of asphalt and parking lines.
- *Corrective maintenance:* Seal cracks, repair potholes and broken sections, repair berms, reline, etc.
- *Charge to restoration and replacement reserve:* Application of new layer of asphalt over entire major section such as one defined lot.

Carpeting

- *Preventive maintenance:* Periodic vacuuming and cleaning.
- *Corrective maintenance:* Replacement of small sections at door entrances and other heavily trafficked areas.
- *Charge to restoration and replacement reserve:* Replacement of carpeting in rooms, hallway, or entire floor level.

Figure 13.2 presents a schedule illustrating an example of the restoration and replacement reserve model used to determine the annual current fund transfer to the plant fund.

Year	Beginning Reserve Balance[a]	Reserve Input at 5.0%[b]	Expenditure Projected Value[c]	Ending Reserve Balance Before Income[d]	Investment Income at 10.00%[e]	Ending Reserve Balance[f]	Future Years Expenditures in Reserve[g]
1993	5,682,416	1,025,000	1,185,840	5,521,576	560,200	6,081,776	3.46
1994	6,081,776	1,076,250	2,185,631	4,972,395	552,709	5,525,103	3.31
1995	5,525,103	1,130,063	55,825	5,988,341	575,672	6,564,013	3.43
1996	6,564,013	1,186,566	2,185,263	5,565,315	606,466	6,171,782	3.87
1997	6,171,782	1,245,894	2,285,123	5,132,553	565,217	5,697,769	3.47
1998	5,697,769	1,308,189	1,263,285	5,742,673	572,022	6,314,695	2.99
1999	6,314,695	1,373,598	1,925,784	5,762,509	603,860	6,366,369	2.75
2000	3,366,369	1,442,278	802,858	7,005,789	668,608	7,674,397	3.16
2001	7,674,397	1,514,392	3,612,483	5,576,306	662,535	6,238,841	3.82
2002	6,238,841	1,590,111	2,612,518	5,216,435	572,764	5,789,199	3.52
2003	5,789,199	1,669,617	1,225,028	6,233,788	601,149	6,834,937	3.13
2004	6,834,937	1,753,098	1,385,652	7,202,383	701,866	7,904,249	2.87
2005	7,904,249	1,840,753	1,245,725	8,499,276	820,176	9,319,453	2.74
2006	9,319,453	1,932,790	3,752,849	7,499,394	840,942	8,340,336	2.67
2007	8,340,446	2,029,430	3,352,125	7,017,641	767,899	7,785,540	2.68
2008	7,785,540	2,130,901	2,985,236	6,931,206	735,837	7,667,043	2.84
2009	7,667,043	2,237,446	2,986,135	6,918,354	729,270	7,674,624	3.12
2010	7,674,624	2,349,319	2,658,521	7,338,422	749,302	7,087,724	3.13
2011	7,087,724	2,466,785	2,396,725	8,157,784	812,275	8,970,059	2.76
2012	8,970,059	2,590,124	2,252,185	9,307,998	913,903	10,221,901	3.22
2013	10,221,901	2,719,630	2,747,994	10,193,537	1,020,772	11,214,309	3.22
2014	11,214,309	2,855,612	5,221,140	8,848,781	1,003,155	9,851,935	3.00
2015	9,851,935	2,998,392	1,530,218	11,320,110	1,058,602	12,378,712	NA
2016	12,378,712	3,148,312	3,358,529	12,168,495	1,227,360	13,395,855	NA
2017	13,395,855	3,305,727	4,969,874	11,731,708	1,256,378	12,988,087	NA

SCHEDULE ILLUSTRATING THE HYPOTHETICAL UNIVERSITY RESTORATION AND REPLACEMENT RESERVE MODEL

FIGURE 13.2

[a]The reserve balance at the end of the previous year. The original balance is established as a nonmandatory fund transfer from operations the year the reserve is created.

[b]Annual nonmandatory transfer from the current fund to the reserve in the plant funds.

[c]Expenditures by year in this column have been adjusted for inflation to reflect expected cost of projects in year performed.

[d]Beginning Reserve Balance, plus Reserve Input, less Expenditure Projected Value.

[e]Expected income on investment of average reserve balance during the year.

[f]Ending Reserve Balance before Income, plus Investment Income.

[g]Number of future years Expenditure Projected Value. Divide expenditures into Ending Reserve Balance. (It's good policy to always have three years in reserve.)

Figure 13.3 is a graph that plots Reserve Input and Expenditures, to demonstrate one of the purposes of the restoration and replacement reserve, which is to smooth the financial demand on current operations as adjusted for inflation.

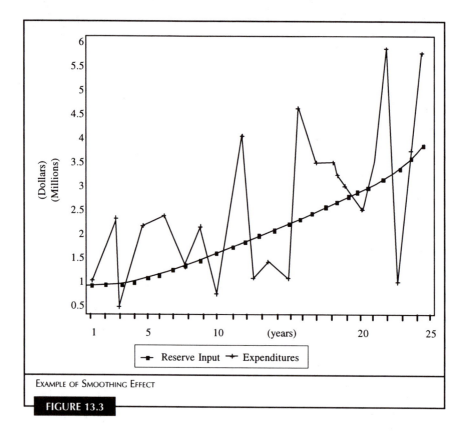

EXAMPLE OF SMOOTHING EFFECT

FIGURE 13.3

Maintaining physical plant construction at a minimum to avoid unwarranted costs requires an extraordinary amount of planning. Following are the highlights of planning activities on campus that directly or indirectly affect the type of space, amount of space for each type, and appropriate maintenance of that space.

CLASSROOM BUILDINGS

Planning for classroom space is probably the most complicated aspect of physical plant management because of the many variations of classrooms, common utilization by various schools in many cases, and the services and amenities available in the individual rooms. A difficult problem is overall usage. If faculty and students had their choice, most classes would be held between 10:00 A.M. and 3:00 P.M. on Tuesday, Wednesday, and Thursday. Obviously, if these choices were translated into policy, classroom facilities required for peak times would be grossly excessive and cost ineffective. Complicating this situation is the fact that the mix of classroom types changes every semester, certainly on an annual basis. Classroom variables include, as a minimum, interactive/traditional/laboratory configurations, number of seats, presence or lack of air-conditioning, and presence or lack of electronic features for voice, video, and data.

A convenient and cost-effective means of addressing the class size variable is to have movable walls for changing the configuration of classrooms as is done in hotel conference centers. In this summary, it is clear that planning of classroom loading regarding the hours in the days and the days in the week, in combination with various sizes and types of classrooms available, is extremely important for convenience of operation as well as minimization of facilities and concomitant costs.

RESIDENCE BUILDINGS

Campus housing has as many facility variables as classrooms, if not more. However, there is greater flexibility in dealing with students as to type of housing facility to which they can be assigned; variances in price according to locality; amenities; and accommodations that provide flexibility regarding student satisfaction and uniform facility utilization. In other words, it is good business to set room rates according to the popularity of accommodations, and to reevaluate price as often as necessary to maintain a relatively uniform demand for the mix of units available.

Residence facilities offer the traditional separation between dormitories, which are basically communal living configurations with sleeping quarters separate from the bathroom facilities, and apartments with self-contained sleeping quarters, kitchen, and dining and living spaces. In recent years, a new form of housing has evolved, which is the townhouse, a hybrid of the two accommodations providing communal living with living/studying/sleeping pods or complexes, serviced by common bathroom facilities.

Planning in the residence area centers around assurance that there will be adequate housing for all students at the start of school in September. However, the overall demand, particularly the mix between dorm facilities and apartments, is also important. This mix not only affects student satisfaction but also affects how much food service the institution must provide. Although all students in dorm accommodations must have board accommodations, most students in apartment accommodations prepare their own meals.

OFFICE SPACE

Planning for office space is probably the easiest of the three major types of space because administrators and faculty do not necessarily have to be in any certain facility, and the mix of personnel changes infrequently. Planning should maximize the proximity of people to the constituency they serve, as well as provide the comfort and amenities required to maintain a happy, productive professional organization. Executive offices, admissions, fund-raising operations, and other marketing-oriented operations should be front, center, and first class.

PARKING FACILITIES

Planning for vehicle parking affects all constituencies—student, faculty, staff, and visitors. Planning for parking in an urban area is particularly difficult because space is limited and parking made available to the various constituencies usually depends on status, which is always a delicate matter. Even in a rural or suburban area, where there is adequate space, parking problems exist. Planners are often faced with unrealistic student/employee expectations for parking spaces close to the building door they normally enter. Under any arrangement, parking is expensive and requires continuous attention and study.

To whatever extent possible, parking should be structured so that it is in close proximity to the primary building of various constituencies. Students in residence should be restricted, where possible, to parking in the residential area and either walk or bike to the academic/administrative areas of the campus to avoid creating a dual parking demand. Parking spaces should be lined to recognize the fact that the average automobile today is considerably smaller than 25 years ago. Parking regulations should be enforced to ensure that those who park legally are not inconvenienced by those individuals who do not.

Below are some simple rules to follow for keeping the investment in parking facilities to a minimum:

- No reserved parking. Space is empty approximately 80 percent of the week and requires diplomatic management, which is expensive.
- No freshman parking for resident students—in the students', parents', and institution's best interest.
- No personal vehicular commuting from residence facilities to classrooms because of the demands placed on designated parking lots.
- No standard versus subcompact parking space because it is impossible to maintain appropriate mix and relative proximity to buildings, and the system discriminates against standard vehicles. Use average-sized lining.

- Avoid a program for charging a parking fee—it appears grasping and requires expensive management. Instead, finance through general revenues. "Free" parking is an excellent marketing feature for students and employees.

FACILITY PLANNING

The planning that goes into various elements of the physical plant is an integral part of the institution's long-term strategic planning responsibilities. Over the years institutional research in the physical plant area should allow the organization to accumulate many ratios, statistics, and substantive analyses that will serve to support the projection of facility needs when an institution is involved in a long-term plan. While mistakes made in planning for personnel resulting from an unforeseen downsizing of the institution can be corrected by workforce reduction, attrition, or retraining, the same cannot be said about the physical plant, particularly if the campus is self-contained. It is difficult to take excess capacity on a campus and sell or lease that space to third parties for other purposes. Mistakes made in the planning of physical facility requirements are costly and, to a great extent, irreversible.

FACILITY DESIGN

A truly cost-effective program for the physical plant starts with the design and construction of the facilities. Construction costs can be reduced by careful attention to plant layout and materials used, while still achieving the quality, efficiency, and aesthetics desired. This is particularly true of the HVAC system (Heat, Ventilation, and Air Conditioning). The era of inexpensive fossil fuel has apparently come to an end, so considerable attention should be given to ensure that HVAC systems are designed and built at minimum cost, yet are still energy efficient. A good system maintains a fine balance between the comfort of the personnel in the facilities and the efficiency of the system. The application of the computer for energy control systems is more important than ever.

The construction of facilities requires two forms of long-range planning to determine the facility needs of all constituencies and detailed planning for proper building layout to achieve the many ambitions for the structure.

OPERATIONAL MAINTENANCE

A cost-efficiency program that is frequently neglected during periods when money is tight is preventive maintenance. Maintenance costs in all facilities can be significantly reduced with an appropriate preventative maintenance program. Preventative maintenance is the first line of defense in a three-phase maintenance program, which also includes corrective maintenance and, eventually, restoration and replacement of facility components. Preventive maintenance is the periodic examination of a system with such appropriate service as replacement of belts, oiling, calibrating, replacement of parts, and general inspection for wear and safety. If a building system is properly maintained through preventative maintenance, corrective procedures can be delayed and costs thereby reduced. In addition, a system breakdown and the cost of temporary alternatives can usually be avoided.

Corrective maintenance is a matter of fixing something after it has broken. Eventually, frequent correction of a broken system becomes cost ineffective, as well as inconvenient, and signals the need for restoration or replacement.

A WORK ORDER COST SYSTEM

A comprehensive maintenance program requires a proper system for management of resources. Every preventive and corrective action taken by trades personnel requires direction. The direction must include description of the problem, assignment of personnel, identification of materials required, and scheduling of the work to be accomplished. Here is yet another application for the computer in the development of an orderly system for identifying and accumulating the thousands of work orders that will be required in a particular period of the year. If a program is going to be developed to accomplish the physical work, it only makes sense that the same program should be used to collect cost by work order for proper distribution and monitoring of maintenance expenditures. Outlined below is a physical plant work order cost system.

System should collect the following information:
- Repetitive preventive maintenance schedule
- Description of corrective work to be accomplished and location
- Priority of corrective work, particularly if life threatening

Physical plant management will:
- Establish a priority for the work
- Determine if the work can be performed in-house or should be subcontracted
- Estimate the various trades involved and hours of effort
- Determine materials required for the order
- Estimate cost of required material, labor, and overhead to complete the order

The computer will:
- Summarize costs for each order

- Summarize labor by trade for backlog determination
- Provide aging of various work orders to determine the viability of the backlog
- Batch work orders by building and location for efficient assignment to trades

Based on above, Physical Plant personnel will:
- Develop a work schedule for trades personnel
- Order material or requisition parts from inventory for work order
- Assign work orders to individual trades personnel

Finally, the computer will:
- Summarize actual cost of material, labor, and overhead against estimates and compute variances
- Summarize cost for maintenance by building
- Summarize material requisitions from inventory for reconciliation to inventory balance

The Work Order Cost System is an effective management tool. It can be used to monitor costs by building or by type of maintenance, serve as an overview on labor backlogs to be used for determining number of tradespeople required, and determine overtime and the proper use of subcontract effort to provide relief to internal support. It can be used by the institutional research staff for developing parametric maintenance relationships to be used in long-range planning. The same system can also be used to accumulate preventive maintenance data based on time intervals, or time run, for various pieces of equipment with automatic issuance of preventive maintenance orders.

A SPACE MANAGEMENT PROGRAM

The final section of this chapter addresses excess facility capacity. In order to maintain a continuous assessment of excess space, a program must be established for space management.

The first step in building a space management program is to maintain up-to-date "as built" schematics of all structures. Properly maintained records will include, at a minimum, type of space, dimensions, utilities (including electronics), built-in facilities, and lighting, power, and wall configurations (to accommodate space reconfiguration options).

Second, with an up-to-date "as built" database, a space inventory program can be designed to include current room utilization and capacity statistics.

Third, current utilization of individual rooms can be computed against maximum capacity data to determine utilization percentages. Examples would be classroom seat utilization by section or office workstation utilization by room.

Fourth, space use can be managed to assure maximum utilization of existing space, rearrangement opportunities to address required changes, assessment of added capacity needs, and determination of possible excess capacity.

Fifth, cost data for depreciation, maintenance, custodial needs, and utilities can be added to the program to establish space cost assignment by cost center. (Use of these data was outlined in Chapter 6.)

EXCESS FACILITY CAPACITY

Institutions will accumulate excess capacity as downsizing continues through most of the 1990s. Floor space is an area where one of Murphy's many laws applies—"Need expands to fill available floor space." Again, we run into the old bugaboo in higher education, which is incremental costing. The attitude can be that as long as the space is available and paid for, it may as well be used. However, space utilization should always be kept to a minimum because available space can possibly be put to a better use in another endeavor.

Identify excess space, and, at the minimum, consider the following options:

- Provide additional offerings in the academic or auxiliary enterprise area if there is a market demand.
- Acquire an academic discipline or school from another institution and absorb it into your own facilities. Sell or lease resultant excess capacity.
- Consider offering courses on a year-round basis. This will increase annual revenues derived from all sources, ensure better utilization of physical facilities, and provide a marketing enticement to students who wish to accelerate the education process. Possibly offer an undergraduate degree in three years, with an option to complete a master's degree in four years. Both the customer and the institution win.
- Use the excess area to realize additional revenues by providing conferencing and special events accommodations to outside organizations.
- Sell or lease the surplus facilities to a third party.
- Merge the entire institution with another institution, and sell or lease excess capacity.
- Mothball a facility until there is a future need.

In addition to the above suggestions, institutions contemplating expansion might want to investigate whether properly managed or renovated existing facilities could meet anticipated needs and thus avoid the cost of facility expansion. As the number of 18-year-olds available to attend college declined, many institutions realized excess capacity. Unless this issue is addressed, students will have to pay for the excess in their tuition rates.

This chapter has discussed the more difficult responsibilities of physical plant management related to construction and maintenance of facilities. In addition, two other functions are traditionally found within the physical plant operation: the day-to-day housekeeping required for internal purposes within the facilities and the external functions for grounds upkeep. Custodial and grounds functions have a tremendous impact on the well-being, happiness, and safety of all personnel. These two functions are considerably less labor intensive than they were in the past because of modern equipment and time-saving techniques. Not only does housekeeping ensure the attractive appearance of a facility, but it is also a key part of a good preventive maintenance program. For instance, a dirty carpet will wear out much faster than a clean one.

Clean, orderly, safe, and aesthetically pleasing buildings and grounds can improve the productivity of students and employees, enhance retention, and serve as a powerful marketing feature.[2] This, in combination with a cost-effective program for construction, maintenance, and maximum utilization of facilities, will strengthen one of the three institutional resources requiring management—the physical plant.

FOR FURTHER READING

Castaldi, Basil. *Educational Facilities: Planning, Remodeling, and Management*. Boston: Allyn and Bacon, Inc., 1977.

College and University Business Administration. 3d ed. Washington, DC: National Association of College and University Business Officers, 1974, 109–35.

Contracting for Facilities Services, No. 9 in Critical Issues in Facilities Management Series, (Association for Physical Plant Administrators), Alexandria, VA, foreword by Sean C. Rush, 1995.

Kaiser, Harvey. *The Facilities Audit*. Alexandria, VA: Association for Physical Plant Administrators, 1994.

Managing the Facilities Portfolio. Washington, DC: National Association of College and University Business Officers, 1991.

Robinson, Daniel D. *Capital Maintenance for Colleges and Universities*. Washington, DC: National Association of College and University Business Officers, 1986.

---

[2]*College and University Business Administration* 3d ed. (Washington, DC: National Association of College and University Business Officers, 1974), 113.

CHAPTER

Financial Aid and Other Subsidies

The GI bill was the quintessential scholarship grant program that promoted higher education for all veterans of World War II and gave impetus to the incredible academic/economic development the country has enjoyed for 50 years.[1] Financial aid was the engine that drove development of higher education in the United States and opened its education opportunities to a broad cross-section of our population.

By the late 1950s, the GI bill had fostered other grant programs as well as debt programs for subsidizing the cost of higher education. The GI bill did not discriminate on the basis of color, ethnic background, wealth, or relative intelligence and academic performance in high school. Of singular interest is the fact that the program also did not discriminate against institutions on the basis of tuition price. Veterans received a fixed subsidy, which they were free to use at any institution of their choice. The cost of an education was subsidized by the taxpayers, and institutions that incurred higher costs with a commensurate higher tuition were supported at exactly the same dollar amount as the lower-cost, lower-tuition institutions.

A broad definition of financial aid is in order here. Financial aid is monies provided either in the form of grants, loans, or work study programs that are available for a student to pay in part or in total the costs of attending an institution of higher education. Costs to the student include tuition and fees, room and board, books, and certain personal expenses. There are two types of financial aid: need based and non-need based. In calculating the amount of a student's need for need-based financial aid, an institution first determines the

---

[1]Arthur M. Hauptman, *The Tuition Dilemma* (Washington, DC: The Brookings Institution, 1990), 65.

amount of money that the student and his or her parents can provide based on their personal wealth and available income. Figure 14.1 illustrates, in a broad context, how such financial aid is determined.

College Cost	Tuition and fees	$10,000	
	Room and board	4,000	
	Other costs/expenses	1,000	$15,000
Aid Sources	Personal resources	$ 4,000	
	External grants and loans	5,000	
	Subtotal	9,000	
	Required internal institutional funds	$ 6,000	$15,000

DETERMINING FINANCIAL AID NEED

FIGURE 14.1

In this simplified example, the institution "recruited" the student by working with the student and parents to fill their financial need. The parents had $4,000 a year available to pay toward expenses. The institution worked with the family to solicit another $5,000 in grants and loans from external sources for a total of $9,000. The institution then provided the student with $6,000 in institutional funds to fully fund the $15,000 required for the student to attend the institution. This oversimplified example is typical of most financial aid arrangements based on financial need. In this example, the $6,000 "gap" between what the student and parents could arrange and the total expense of $15,000 was closed by the institution. Sometimes, however, the institution cannot fill the gap completely. If a gap is left open, the institution is taking the risk that the student will enroll at another institution that will reduce the gap or close it completely. Using the above example, the institution opens its doors to the general population independent of personal financial circumstances, if the student satisfies the basic academic criteria.

"Non-need-based" financial aid is used to build a diverse student body by providing full or substantial institutional scholarship to a variety of targeted students. Examples include minority students with strong academic potential, varsity athletes, and merit students who have their pick of institutions. Non-need-based financial aid is provided without knowledge of the student's financial circumstance. Wealthy, meritorious, and athletic students receive the same amount as the "needy."

This chapter focuses on institutional financial aid in particular because it is the only form of financial aid over which the institution has complete control.

But before discussing institutional financial aid, which is realized by means of tuition price discounting, we should place in perspective the many forms of aid available to students that culminate in a price that is significantly less than the true cost of education, particularly at state institutions.

OVERVIEW OF PUBLIC FINANCIAL SUBSIDY TO HIGHER EDUCATION

The financial support of higher education is achieved by six methods of subsidy—tax exemption, government and organization support, external financial aid, cost avoidance, working capital enhancements, and internal financial aid.

Tax Exemption

As a not-for-profit organization, institutions of higher education are exempt from paying taxes on activities that are education related.

Government and Organization Support

The original form of subsidy to higher education was government land grants for establishing campuses. Land grant institutions were then developed and perpetuated by state, private, and religious organizations. Eventually, cities began to participate in government-supported higher education.

When you consider that approximately half of the institutions of higher education in the United States are state or organization supported[2] and 80 percent of state institution expenses are subsidized by tax dollars,[3] it is obvious that conservatively 40 percent (one-half of 80 percent) of all institution costs in the United States are subsidized by state income and sales taxes. I use the term *conservatively* because a larger proportion of state institutions are major universities.

External Financial Aid

External financial aid is granted students from government agencies, foundations, and other third-party participants. The subsidy, whether run through the institution's books or paid directly to the student, subsidizes the student and not the institution. Third-party giving also includes grants and loans from the institution's endowments. Strange as it seems, the assets of a scholarship's endowment belong to the institution but the earnings from the endowment

---

[2]Peter Likins, "Doing More with Less," *EACUBO Newsletter* (Winter 1992): 6.

[3]Arthur M. Hauptman, *The Tuition Dilemma* (Washington, DC: The Brookings Institution, 1990), 5.

are distributed to the students. (As price becomes more of a competitive issue in the future, scholarship endowments will become more important. They will permit the institution to contain tuition price because the endowment scholarships can displace part of the discounting requirement, which increases tuition price.)

Cost Avoidance

This category of subsidy provides funds that allow an institution to avoid spending its own capital and to maintain a lower tuition rate. Such subsidies can include:

- Gifts of buildings and capital items
- Gifts to establish endowments that provide funds for faculty chairs and enrichment programs
- Gifts for academic program development
- Gifts of physical plant or other services

Working Capital Enhancements

Various earnings enhancements are available to generate working capital on activities independent of classroom instruction and research. They are legally within the charter of the not-for-profit business entity. Examples include:

- Annual giving for general operations
- The transfer of earnings on quasi-endowments for use in supporting general operations
- Earnings on working capital
- Earnings on auxiliary enterprises — room, board, food service, bookstore, etc.
- Earnings on education-related ancillary activities

After reviewing the first five of the six forms of financial subsidies to higher education, it is obvious that higher education is heavily subsidized. This is certainly not a condition conducive to productivity and cost efficiency during centuries of rapid growth and expansion.

Internal Financial Aid

This form of financial aid is theoretically a transfer of tuition cost among student groups.

Transfer of tuition cost among students is realized by means of discounting. Specifically, the tuition rate charged all students is increased sufficiently to enable the institution to discount in whole or in part tuition charged to selected students. In effect, the full-pay students pay a portion of the tuition for the needy, as well as targeted minority, varsity athletic, and merit students. (This form of financial aid will be reviewed in depth later in this chapter.)

FINANCIAL AID AND STRATEGIC PLANNING

Financial aid and its judicial application are inseparable from the strategic planning required to properly market an institution. Even after the demographic decline in students stabilizes in 1996, financial aid will take on greater importance in the strategy to maintain, or improve, the prestige of an institution by controlling the quality of its student body while making maximum effort to maintain tuition revenues.[4] A reasonable revenue base will be required to continue programs in place and support the heavy fixed costs of the institution.

The use of financial aid in marketing will be a challenge during the 1990s because of the shrinking number of students, exacerbated by the pressure to hold annual tuition increases at the level of inflation, or less, while remaining competitive in a price-sensitive marketplace. One does not have to be an accountant to know that if business is decreasing in both volume and rate, and there is the ambition to increase discounting for financial aid, a problem of monumental proportions will develop.

Marketing strategy regarding the disposition of financial aid will center around achieving the mission of the institution while maintaining the quality and quantity of students desired, maintaining student selectivity while protecting the diversity desired, aligning the institution to successfully compete against the competition, and, finally, achieving "all of the above" while maintaining financial viability. Success in pursuing this endeavor will depend in large part on the ability of the board of trustees to attract business-oriented officers who understand the higher education industry and are able to manage the institution as a business.

Pricing and discounting in higher education during the 1990s will be particularly troublesome as a result of the following circumstances:

- The United States has entered a highly competitive global marketplace.
- Higher education aggressively increased tuition rates in the latter part of the 1970s and throughout the 1980s.
- The demographic decline will continue until 1996 and then rise only slowly for the next 18 years.
- Education costs have become unmanageable for most of the American public.[5]

---

[4]Sandra L. Johnson and Joel W. Meyerson, "More Top Concerns for 1992," *AGB Reports* (January/February 1992): 12.

[5]Arthur M. Hauptman, *The Tuition Dilemma* (Washington, DC: The Brookings Institution, 1990), 2-5.

For the above reasons, it will be impossible to continue to increase discounting as a percentage of tuition at the exponential rate it increased during the past 10 years. Either the discount rate will have to stabilize or higher education will have to (1) make unheard of reductions in the cost of delivering its product, (2) create means of making higher education less dependent on tuition as a source of revenue, or (3) make dramatic improvements in productivity.

Each year, management must decide how much of a discount it will provide relative to the percentage of increase in tuition. If the tuition discount is increased an amount that exceeds the revenues realized on the tuition rate increase, net revenue flow from tuition will decrease. In a period of level or declining enrollments, such as is being experienced now, the amount of discount is particularly critical because gross revenues from year to year are declining while fixed costs remain level and inflation continues to batter variable costs. The burden of financing the discounts will shift from the wealthy student to the institution, resulting in narrowing margins and, eventually, deficits. Figure 14.2 illustrates this scenario.

As shown in Figure 14.2, costs do not change appreciably as tuition rate increases subside and financial aid discounts increase. This problem is created by management attempting to "buy" enrollment volume with ever heavier

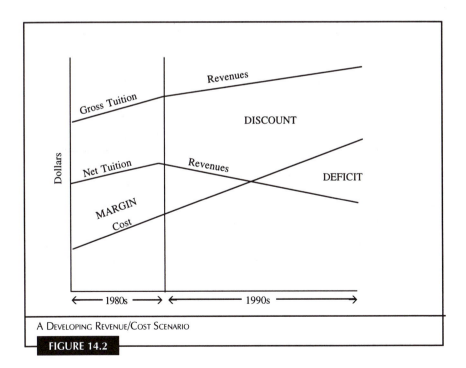

A Developing Revenue/Cost Scenario

FIGURE 14.2

price discounts. There will be a temptation to rationalize the belief that securing $10,000 in revenue is worth any discount up to the $10,000.

This type of strategy will only hasten the rush to deficit spending because sustained enrollment volume will make it difficult, if not impossible, to reduce variable cost and impossible to make appropriate disposition of excess capacity and other fixed cost. An institution should remain financially viable to best serve its societal mission. If there are fewer students to serve, downsize the institution and downsize the industry of higher education.

If it is true that families face difficulty paying for the cost of higher education, then there will be fewer students to charge more tuition to pay for the greater number of students who will have need—a developing point of diminishing returns as shown in Figure 14.2. Tuition discounting has become a major planning strategy, and, unfortunately, has become many institutions' "Waterloo" in the 1990s.

Who are these people who administer financial aid and fashion the student body? A professional director of financial aid or enrollment manager must be the master of a high-wire act to manage properly the many variables and statistical probabilities that must be balanced in order to achieve a desired student profile while not overruning the institution's allotted funds for financial aid discounting.

MANAGEMENT CRITERIA FOR A FINANCIAL AID PROGRAM

The many considerations that must be addressed to satisfy management's criteria for a financial aid program will be reviewed individually but not necessarily in order of importance. Importance is properly based on the strategy developed by management at those institutions using financial aid as a marketing tool and the priorities established to achieve those strategies. These variables and statistical probability considerations are discussed below.

Student Profile Regarding Diversity

Discretionary institution funds for financial aid are used to achieve diversity in the student body based on minority, athletics, and academic factors. Funds set aside for specific "target" groups are allocated as part or full tuition and, in some cases, also include room and board. Full tuition cost allows an institution to target for recruitment a specific number of students in a designated category. Partial subsidy allows the institution to slant enrollments toward the desired diversity composition.

Discount Required for Retention for Continuing Students, Relative to Discount Required for Recruitment

Financial aid must be carefully balanced between the amount allocated for the admission of new students and the amount required to retain continuing students. When enrollments decline, institutions will be tempted to allocate an inordinate amount of funds to attract new students, while reducing their support to continuing students. If additional debt is available to continuing students, the temptation will be to "bait and switch." In this scenario institutional funds are provided to attract students, but once they enroll, they find themselves financing their second and subsequent years more with debt and personal funds than with institutional funds.

Marketing extends to the total student body, not just to recruiting. It will behoove an institution to balance carefully recruiting and retention to realize maximum enrollment while treating fairly the entire student body.

Quality versus Quantity in Enrollment

The distribution of institution financial aid provides an opportunity to balance student enrollment between quality and quantity. If the institution is willing to sacrifice some quality to achieve a higher enrollment level, institutional funds can be used to finance students who have financial need but may also have weak academic credentials.[6] The demographic problem will pressure many institutions to trade off some quality to keep their enrollment and revenue flow at a higher level.

Societal Desires versus Institutional Needs versus Country's Needs

The institution must consider the tradeoffs among society's desires for average and minority students to be educated; the institution's needs to maintain quality, minimize the costs of discounting, and support programs; and the country's competitive need for the brightest and best to receive a solid education. To attempt to serve all during a period of retrenchment can adversely affect quality standards, diversification of the institution's ambitions, and financial outlook. It's a catch-22 in a difficult market. For example, sacrificing quality and becoming an open admissions institution is suicide for a private organization if it has a high tuition rate in combination with a high discount rate.[7]

---

[6]Kent John Chabotar and James P. Honan, "Coping with Retrenchment: Strategies and Tactics," *Change* (November/December 1990): 30.

[7]Nathaniel H. Karol and Sigmund G. Ginsburg, *Managing the Higher Education Enterprise* (New York: John Wiley & Sons, Inc., 1980), 2.

Change in Marketing Strategy

After a number of years, an institution might find its recruiting drifting away from the quality, diversity, or other market criteria the institution had established to satisfy its mission. It is also possible that the competition might change its strategy, forcing your institution to make a change. This introduces the problem of allocating financial aid required for continued recruitment of students based on the old mission versus a redistribution of funds for recruiting students designated to be more in line with a revised mission and strategy.

Debt versus Grant Financial Aid

The most desirable form of financial aid is a grant. However, financial aid packages are assembled with a considerable amount of debt. Because institutional financial aid, in the form of discounting, is grant money, it provides the institution with the opportunity to determine both total funds offered, as well as adjusting the balance between grant and debt. All things being equal, if competing institutions are offering the same "gap" between total costs and total financial assistance, the institution that provides the greatest amount of grant relative to debt will have the edge in marketing.

Financial Aid Offered versus Financial Aid Accepted

The last and most difficult balancing act of distributing institution financial aid is the requirement to statistically second-guess how much aid, in each category provided, will finally be required to recruit the incoming freshman class. The balance is achieved by reviewing the statistics for prior years regarding the number of students who agreed to attend an institution after they were accepted, and the aid package designed for their use.[8] This analysis must be made for each category (i.e., general aid, minority, varsity, merit, etc.).

The financial aid office must second-guess the mix of aid given each student who has been extended an invitation to attend, which students will attend, and how many students will fit into each institutional aid category to avoid an overrun of total funds provided. In many instances, the financial aid office is offering twice as much money as is available in any given category on the belief that the final student yield will approximate the funds budgeted for that particular category and that the sum of the "approximates" for each category will not exceed total funds provided.

Many institutions are unaware of the extraordinary financial exposure they have in this area if the financial aid office is not properly managed.

---

[8]*Management of Student Aid* (Washington, DC: National Association of College and University Business Officers, 1979), 36.

With this introduction to the basics of financial aid, we are now ready to review institution tuition discounting in the 1990s. Thus far, we have reviewed tuition discounting in relation to recruitment and retention of students. There is a second category of discounting: tuition remission. Unlike financial aid, tuition remission is used to recruit and retain employees rather than students. Tuition remission is an established and accepted employee fringe benefit in higher education. Students are the end result because the entitlement for the employees allows them to enjoy total or partial tuition discounts for themselves as well as their dependents. Tuition remission is considered necessary to attract and retain the brightest and best faculty/administration.[9]

The balance of this chapter is devoted to explaining in-depth how tuition discounting is determined, and its use and application in the marketing of the institution. Tuition discounting is significant because in some institutions it can amount to 50 percent or more of total financial aid available to the student body.[10]

TUITION DISCOUNTING

Financial Aid

Internal financial aid seeks to create a predetermined level of student enrollment and diversity. (This form of subsidy to higher education was discussed earlier in this chapter.) It is segregated into budgets designated by financial need, merit, minority recruitment, and varsity athletics. Budgets are further broken down into funds for recruitment of new students and retention of students currently attending the institution.

Institutional funds for financial aid are generally used to pay for tuition and room and board, or tuition only. These funds are used to close the "gap" between the total cost of attending the institution and a student's individual financial resources, including personal, governmental, and other private sources of financial aid.

Tuition Remission

Tuition remission seeks to attract and retain employees by offering them, their spouses, and their dependents free or reduced tuition. If dependents are academically qualified, they are guaranteed admission. When employees use it for their own education, tuition remission serves to support the institution's training and employee development programs. Unfortunately, it is generally

---

[9]Howard R. Bowen, *The Costs of Higher Education: How Much Do Colleges and Universities Spend Per Student and How Much Should They Spend?* (San Francisco: Jossey-Bass, Inc., 1980), 66.

[10]Kent John Chabotar and James P. Honan, "Coping with Retrenchment: Strategies and Tactics," *Change* (November/December 1990): 30.

viewed as an inexpensive means to provide a valuable and highly competitive fringe benefit. However, it is difficult to budget tuition remission because as a fringe benefit it is an entitlement, and the institution has no way of anticipating who will take advantage of the opportunity.

FINANCIAL IMPLICATIONS

Discounting in General

In preparing an institution's operating budget, enrollments are projected and costs are developed to support a budgeted number of students. Total enrollment includes students paying full cost, those receiving full institution scholarships, those receiving tuition subsidies to close the "gap" between the cost of attendance and their financial resources, and students on tuition remission.

Tuition is set at an amount that provides sufficient revenue for an institution to absorb all costs, including the discount deemed necessary to satisfy current market requirements for attracting students and employees. As the tuition discount increases, the amount of tuition charged all students is increased or institution capital is depleted. Figure 14.3 shows a typical experience.

Discounting of tuition for financial aid has increased sharply throughout higher education for the following reasons:

- Tuition rates increased at a double-digit level throughout the 1980s.
- The level of federal and state tuition grants declined during the 1980s as a percentage of total higher education cost and as a percentage of total aid offered.

	(1)	(2)	(3)	(4)	(5)	(6)	(7)
	Tuition Remission	College Financial Aid	Total Discount (1+2)	Total Tuition & Fees	% of Discount to Total Tuition & Fees (3÷4)	Net Tuition & Fees	% Increase From Previous Year
7/1/81–6/30/82	$207,469	$1,117,425	$1,324,894	$21,569,484	6.14%	$20,244,590	–
7/1/82–6/30/83	273,589	1,1517,116	1,790,705	24,440,658	7.33%	22,649,953	11.9%
7/1/83–6/30/84	269,955	2,205,360	2,475,315	29,126,251	8.50%	26,650,936	10.5%
7/1/84–6/30/85	274,078	2,745,404	3,019,482	32,480,546	9.30%	29,461,064	10.5%
7/1/85–6/30/86	304,198	3,288,268	3,592,466	34,583,888	10.39%	30,991,422	5.2%
7/1/86–6/30/87	471,843	3,853,550	4,325,393	37,666,725	11.48%	33,341,332	7.6%
7/1/87–6/30/88	621,115	4,515,184	5,136,299	41,912,946	12.25%	36,776,648	10.3%
7/1/88–6/30/89	790,980	5,069,218	5,860,198	47,431,505	12.36%	41,571,307	10.4%
7/1/89–6/30/90	1,057,576	6,129,179	7,199,755	53,074,079	13.54%	45,887,324	10.4%
7/1/90–6/30/91	1,220,000	7,468,000	8,688,000	58,673,000	14.81%	49,985,000	8.9%
7/1/91–6/30/92	1,514,462	7,987,969	9,502,431	59,169,000	16.10%	49,666,569	(.6%)

EXAMPLE OF RECENT TRENDS IN DISCOUNTING AT A HYPOTHETICAL INSTITUTION

FIGURE 14.3

- The 1990s started with a major recession that resulted in widespread layoffs, early retirements, and a slowing of salary increases.
- Students and their parents were forced to accept more aid in the form of debt, resulting in debt capacity limitations.
- The home equity loan was developed to allow the public to borrow against their "estate." This debt form of support is creating debt capacity problems, complicated by declining property values.
- Personal debt for all purposes became burdensome because of credit card abuses.
- The dual-income family phenomenon matured.
- The United States is in the middle of an economic adjustment to step down onto the playing field of a highly competitive, democratic global society. This will have a deleterious impact on wages in the United States for the balance of the decade.
- The demographic decline of high school graduates has resulted in reduced enrollments that tend to force discounting to become a greater percentage of the whole because of the upward pressure on tuition increases to absorb fixed costs.
- Tuition remission in higher education is regarded as a cultural entitlement necessary to compete for qualified employees. Institutions have been generous in granting this benefit.

Discounting is absolutely necessary to compete. Pricing has finally become a significant factor in marketing. The balancing act is to discount just enough to achieve desired quality enrollment/employment goals in a highly competitive marketplace while maintaining the cash flow needed to run the institution.

Similarities Between Financial Aid and Tuition Remission

- Both have dollar-for-dollar impact on budgeted tuition levels. For every dollar of discount the tuition rate is increased, a dollar must be added to the tuition rate to compensate for revenue loss; or tuition is not increased and cash flow is reduced by a dollar.
- Both have the same impact on budgeted cost where individual enrollment is predetermined to be a full or partial reimbursement, such as 25 percent, 50 percent, or 75 percent, because the "classroom seat" is budgeted and costed.
  Both usually have a four-year impact on discounting once committed.

Differences Between Financial Aid and Tuition Remission

- As an entitlement, tuition remission is difficult to budget because the institution does not know which family members will attend, or when they will attend.
- Tuition remission is blind to institutional goals regarding student quality and diversity.

- Unlike tuition remission, which is a fixed amount by benefit entitlement, the portion of financial aid that is not granted to an individual for a budgeted classroom seat can be distributed among many students and used to create student diversity and fill "tuition gaps" to enhance revenue by attracting and retaining additional students to whom the institution would otherwise not be able to extend aid. This item will become a strategy consideration during the next decade as discounts become dear and institutions strive to maintain financial viability.

Financial aid discounts can maximize margin generation relative to tuition remission because, if distributed properly, they maximize the amount of money brought to the institution from other sources available to the students.

Budgeting/Accounting

- Current year discounting activity has an immeasurable impact on revenues and expenses. Tuition rates are established to absorb all or part of the budgeted discount, and faculty staffing/support costs are established to support the budgeted level of enrollment. Therefore, the addition or deletion of a few individual "100% discounted students" would not influence costs one way or another because there are usually seats available within sections. However, when it comes to financial aid for "gapping" purposes, increased discounting over budget to achieve enrollment levels may result in capturing the portion of tuition, room, and board that the students provide from their own financial resources and third-party financial aid. In other words, it could be a judgment call during recruiting and retention to spend a dollar to capture five dollars in revenue that are about to slip away.
- The effect of heavier discounting in the current year has a direct financial implication on subsequent years. The stage is set to increase future rates to absorb the higher level of discounting, which reduces the competitiveness of the institution, or if rates are not adjusted to absorb the added discount, costs must be reduced to make up the difference to avoid deficit spending.
- The cost to support the discount activity of the institution is exactly the same as the cost to support the full tuition sector (i.e., there are no "free" seats). However, as discussed in item 1 of this section, a few wholly discounted students could be added incrementally in a given year with no cost impact because empty seats are usually available. This is true of any business enterprise that has flexible capacity. However, cost, price, and capacity have to be addressed in total and on a continuous year-to-year basis because heavier discount activity

is cumulative. If all constituencies in the discounting programs assumed an incremental approach to their portion of the program, discounting would soon get out of control.

CONCLUSIONS

Higher education is being forced by demographics to downsize its day undergraduate enrollment in a market where the public is having difficulty affording tuition, particularly that of private institutions. Future tuition increases will probably be held to the level of inflation, and "net price" will probably play a greater role in marketing an institution. Declining demographics through the mid-1990s will be complicated by students shifting their fields of interest, particularly women as they return, in part, to more traditional professions.

Higher education is ceasing to be a "cost plus" business, and continued ambitious discounting will be impossible to pass through in pricing as it has been in the past. All sectors of discounting should be monitored carefully to ensure that no more is committed than absolutely necessary to achieve goals. Priorities will have to be continually reset to balance discount goals against marketing position.

To repeat, discounting will become more of a catch-22 if it forces pricing to a level where there are fewer students to pay full tuition to support a growing base of those who receive a discount. It will ultimately create enrollment failures.

A review of financial aid would be incomplete if six controversial subjects that may affect future student aid were not mentioned.

1. There are those who believe students should mortgage their future because higher education is an investment in their personal life that will permit them to realize higher lifetime earnings. Those who propose this program for the purpose of supporting ever-greater tuition rates should review what debt did to the United States in the 1980s. The country successfully extended an unwarranted standard of living through the combination of extraordinary national debt, an extraordinary balance of international payments, a plethora of personal credit card debt, development loans on properties that depreciated, and equity mortgages on homes that depreciated. Mortgaging our children's future is not the answer to higher education's problem.

2. There are those who believe in the "Mercedes Benz" phenomenon regarding pricing, that is, if the tuition is expensive, quality and status must be built in. The government supports it because it provides financial aid in proportion to price; many parents believe it and favor high-priced schools; and certainly higher education believes it because his-

torically it enhanced reputation and cash flow. The belief that quality was associated with price engendered aggressive tuition increases that have contributed to the support of another of Murphy's laws: "Institutional spending will expand to absorb all revenue generated."

3. Minority students will represent a larger percentage of total students attending institutions of higher education by the year 2030. This demographic change will most likely increase demand for financial aid.[11] Pricing will be more difficult during the next decade because it is the spread between sticker price and funds available to pay. The difference is the "gap" that can only be narrowed by tuition discounting or cost containment.

4. If discounting is increased at a faster rate than tuition can be increased to absorb the added cost, margins will decrease as the institution absorbs the discounts. Eventually, deficits will be incurred to support discounting.

5. The tuition remission programs at many institutions are too generous. The benefits offered go far beyond any incentive necessary to compete for talented employees. This will be particularly true through the remainder of the 1990s as higher education is downsized. This benefit entitlement should be reviewed and curtailed. The funds saved could reduce impending deficits or be used as financial aid to recruit students who pay a greater portion of total tuition.

6. If tuition discounts reach the 20 percent to 40 percent level at most institutions, higher education should reduce its sticker prices to avoid scaring the public. A scared public just might decide to refrain from pursuing higher education.

A new era has dawned in higher education for pricing and discounting.

FOR FURTHER READING

Chabotar, Kent John and Honan, James P. "Coping with Retrenchment: Strategies and Tactics." *Change* (November/December, 1990): 28–34.

Hauptman, Arthur M. *The Tuition Dilemma*. Washington, DC: The Brookings Institution, 1990, 2–5.

Hubbel, Loren Loomis, and Sean C. Rush. *A Double-Edged Sword: Assessing the Impact of Tuition Discounting*. Washington, DC: National Association of College and University Business Officers, December 1991.

Hubbel, Loren Loomis. *Tuition Discounting: The Impact of Institutionally Funded Financial Aid*. Washington, DC: National Association of College and University Business Officers, 1992.

---

[11]Martin Kramer, "Money and Race Relations: Toward a Color Blind Financial Aid System," *Change* (May/June 1991): 53-54.

PART
VI

· · · · · · · · · ·

Conclusions and Predictions

CHAPTER 15

Potpourri

I n this concluding chapter, we will tie up the loose ends and uncompleted thoughts. The chapter ends with a summary that lists the author's predictions of unfolding events during the balance of the decade.

MANAGEMENT

Managing human affairs productively requires organization and governance. Higher education has the broad mission of providing the finest education possible at a price that all who have a desire to pursue an education beyond high school can afford. There is a societal mission, and, therefore, the business belongs to the people.

Organizations can be either "administered" or "managed." There is a distinct difference. Governments are administered; businesses are led by managers. Higher education, unfortunately, identifies more with a government than a business. It believes in representation, of faculty, students, and trustees; consensus rather than the vision of a leader; many in charge of direction rather than an individual in charge; provision of functions rather than the development and execution of functions; contributions toward an end rather than development of an end; and presiding over rather than leading or controlling the development of events.

Although the difference in managing as opposed to administrating may appear to be subtle, it is distinctly different. To manage is to direct and control, to make things happen, to conduct the business affairs of the organization. Higher education is not a society that requires a government. It is a business that requires an appointed individual who has leadership skills, has vision, makes skillful use of the means to accomplish a purpose, motivates subordinates to excel, provides the most productivity at minimum cost (value), is an adroit schemer and intriguer, and delivers a quality service to the customer. Unless higher education aligns itself as a business and appoints management personnel, identifying them as managers rather than administrators, costs will continue to escalate as they do in government. Higher education will be available only to a wealthy minority.

PROFIT VERSUS EXCESS OF REVENUES OVER EXPENDITURES AND MANDATORY TRANSFERS

If you use the above ten-word expression to describe profit, you are politically and legally correct. It is acceptable to say that your institution has never incurred a deficit, but God help you if you ever say you made a profit. Apparently, what is politically correct in terms of performance is to break even each and every year. It is time to talk openly about the business affairs of higher education, particularly the private sector, which is not directly subsidized by any government or organization.

There is a need for institutions to earn a profit for capital formation. In fact, most institutions do earn a profit and quietly shuffle it between funds. If they did not earn a profit and reinvest it in the business to develop, they would still be at the starting gate financially. My recommendations for bringing profit making by higher education out of the closet are to (1) redesignate higher education as tax-exempt rather than not-for-profit and (2) allow higher education to earn a profit and combine it with a judicial mix of debt and anticipated gifts to manage its affairs. If the profit is not required to meet expenditures, it can be reinvested in the institution and used to accommodate the mission of maintaining tuition at a minimum.

HUMAN VALUES—BUSINESS VALUES

Old-fashioned business "rules" are being reincarnated throughout the United States. The 1980s proved how low some government and business leaders had sunk in their personal and professional conduct. Apparently they forgot everything they learned in the home and at church, or were unable to compete in a world ethically, so they resorted to unfair practices. The Golden Rule has been resurrected and business is preaching values in the form of ethics, quality, and frugality—practices that will restore the nation's competitiveness and make everyone feel good.

Basic values that were once taught during the developmental stages of childhood in the home are now being taught in the office; better late than never. Higher education recognizes the need for ethics in business and is pursuing developmental programs in ethics education, TQM (Total Quality Management) education, and cost reduction/containment applications. Although the programs have not been grouped under a common program of "value, identity, and development," they are being promoted individually, and certainly this addresses the problem on an initial basis. Unfortunately, teaching values in the workplace is an expensive procedure and is not a long-term substitute for regrouping the family and teaching values as a way of life.

I support the teaching of human values and their application in the workplace to produce product value and provide service value. The following is a speech I gave early in 1992 to help launch the college's installation of a formal TQM program. The speech was an attempt to integrate ethics, quality, and frugality in the workplace.

TQM AND THE BUSINESS OF HIGHER EDUCATION
by Robert L. Lenington, 1992

Good afternoon and welcome to the greatest little business school in Massachusetts, Texas, and the other 48 states.

As a former businessman, I view the development of curriculum to be the engineering operation of undergraduate education, and classroom instruction the manufacturing operation. The high school student (and his or her parents) is our customer, the enrolled student our client, and the graduating student our product. TQM is a natural for the education process of an institution.

Quality service for the applicant begins with the recruitment process, including brochures, personal contacts, applications, tour of facilities, followed by acceptance and orientation. Immediately thereafter is the admissions process, financial aid evaluation, residence arrangements, and, ultimately, registration. The customer has to be impressed by appearance, organization, efficiency, and feel that the institution cares. Of course, the science of enrollment management, which is applied TQM, includes attention to student retention and the care needed to ensure that most students graduate four years later.

TQM is not new. The Japanese built junk before World War II, learned from our consultants to build quality after the war, and are beating us at our own game. Witness the recent Bush/Japanese junket with two top American executives asking for relief.

TQM has been packaged over the years as OC, ZD, TQM, TQC, et cetera. In essence, TQM is sound management practice that measures customer satisfaction and communicates specific employee actions that constitute the price/quality trade-offs that will assure a competitive product that sells in quantity—at a profit. If it's a service business like higher education, the same principles apply. These principles provide a quality program delivered to a pleased student, who will absorb instruction, which will place that student in a position to successfully respond to society's needs, delivered by an institution that remains financially viable.

To be competitive, the strategy is to deliver equal quality for less. Again, the Japanese are showing the way. A recent example: BMW 735 and Mercedes Benz 420 automobile owners are trading their vehicles in for Toyota Lexus 400s. Used 735s and 420s are selling for less than book. A new 735 or 420 sells for $60,000. A new Lexus 400 sells for $40,000. Equal performance—equal quality—$20,000 less—no contest. The American public is learning that there is not a guaranteed direct correlation between quality and price—a new understanding is developing called "value."

The Holy Grail of any human endeavor should be excellence, which is quality. TQM is management communicating to its organization quality/ cost standards determined by customer input, probing the standards through evaluation and reports, closing the communication lines through feedback, correcting problems, rewarding the performers, *and arranging for the nonperformers to work for the competition.* Management designed around TQM must be installed as a way of life.

TQM should be applied to all student services throughout the campus from the bursar's office to recreation activities. The student is the customer.

The focal point for TQM in higher education is in the education process. The faculty must develop curriculum and research that is relevant to society's needs, maximize utilization of facilities and equipment available for instruction, attend to individual student needs and problems, and deliver quality education at minimum cost per classroom seat occupied.

If we have developed a quality product for our students, then we will have produced a quality product in our students. They will be offered significant entry-level positions in their respective fields at salaries in excess of those offered students from competitive institutions.

Word will spread that your institution provides a superior product. Applicants will line up at the entrance to your campus recognizing value, and employers will line up at your Office of Career Services recognizing quality.

Our institution embraces the management concepts of TQM. It is our plan to develop a comprehensive set of practices along with a cost system that will identify revenue versus cost through the entire accounting structure with the student sitting in a seat in the classroom as the basis. A system that can be used for margin or loss identity. This will provide a computer program to

- identify by discipline, by school, by college, by day or evening the margins or losses for quality/cost trade-offs, and
- develop online capability for multiyear revenue/cost simulation to study, analyze, and develop long-term institution strategy.

It's a pleasure to provide the services and facilities of our institution today for your workshop. For those of you who have an AACSB-accredited business school, I trust you will embrace TQM in order to remain competitive with our college.

Thank you.

EMPTY CLASSROOM SEATS

If an airplane is committed to fly and there are empty seats, the empty seat costs are fully absorbed and the airline has forgone a revenue. The airlines learned this financial reality a number of years ago and have since attempted to fill the empty seats by discounting tickets for last-minute availability, selling to senior citizens, and providing no-charge tickets for airline employees/ spouses/ parents. The program is on a seat-available basis.

An analogy can be made between the airline industry and higher education. If the decision is made at the time of registration that a sufficient number of students have registered for a section to warrant proceeding with the class, and drop/add has cycled, invariably there are empty seats in the room. The classroom and the faculty member are committed in total.

Why not make the empty seats available to the economically disadvantaged on a "seat-available basis" according to a queuing priority? Admittedly, it would be inconvenient for students on such an education program and would probably extend the four-year cycle for a degree. However, the country could provide a massive shadow education program free to economically disadvantaged students at no cost to participating institutions. I will not discourse any further on the "seat-available basis" concept because it is a potpourri item not germane to the subject of this book. But it is something to at least think about.

SUMMARY

As a final presumptive act, I would like to summarize the book with a list of conclusions and predictions of unfolding events during the next decade.

- Higher education is in trouble regarding cost, delivery of instruction, and attitude of the incumbent professionals who provide the services.
- The American public is paying an excessive price in taxes and tuition for an opportunity that should be available to all citizens who are able to achieve the essential prerequisites for a degree.
- The quantity of committees, studies, analyses, research, articles, and books generated during the 1990s will provide overwhelming evidence that major changes are required in higher education.
- Higher education will be recognized as a major critical industry that must conduct its affairs in a businesslike manner. Management will be strengthened, accounting systems will be structured more like industry to disclose financial performance, and strategic planning will become a reality.
- Values will be identified that will be instilled in the conduct of the employees who operate institutions, and those same values will become an integral part of the curriculum. The values will be simple and serve the country well: ethics, productivity, cost-efficiency, and quality.
- During the process of change, studies will disclose that high school graduates who under normal circumstances would pursue higher learning are not applying because classroom seats are not available in state schools and private education is beyond their financial means. This will be the second demographic "problem" imposed by the higher education industry on itself and society.
- Changes in the industry will accelerate. Institutions will merge or learn to work together to better serve their societal mission of providing an efficient, cost-effective, quality instruction delivery system for the citizens of our country.
- Extended education will become a cost-effective means of delivering instruction. The concept is real because it capitalizes on the use of data communications, eliminates the need for room and board for those who can't afford the luxury, and accommodates the sharing of faculty, facilities, and curriculum between institutions. The methodology will make education possible for the average citizen without the need for an oversized, expensive, inequitable, antiquated, socialistic financial aid structure.
- The practice of heavy discounting of tuition to provide financial aid for athletes, intelligent wealthy, lower-income individuals, children of faculty and staff, and minorities will be reconsidered and redefined. The middle class has finally figured out that it is supporting the country with hard work and the capacity to incur debt. A large portion of our middle class does not qualify for financial aid in the

form of grants. However, these middle class applicants do qualify for financial aid and home equity loans, which support (1) their own children's educations and (2) a subsidy for approximately 50 percent of other parents' children who are provided scholarships and grants through tuition discounts.

- Consortiums of institutions will be formed to provide common pools of activity to take advantage of shared resources, including faculty, facilities, curriculum, materials and supply purchases, energy purchases, data communications, and overseas marketing regarding regional opportunities. In addition, insurance pools will be formed, particularly medical, and outsourcing of services will be pursued to move away from the stagnation of unions and take advantage of the country's downsizing evolution.

- Financial aid discounts will be considered for extention to foreign students. This would improve profit-and-loss statements because the discount provided one American student could buy multiple international students. This survival strategy by some institutions will sacrifice some domestic students, and force American citizens to subsidize the education of foreign students.

- Despite pressures to contain cost and improve productivity, institutions will be forced to allocate 10 percent or more of their budgets to the acquisition and maintenance of electronic technologies.

- Enrollment of foreign students who pay full tuition will decline. Competitive institutions overseas will prevail and increase their market share of foreign students and possibly American students.

- Graduate education, particularly evening programs, will continue to expand as society recognizes that competition for good positions requires an advanced degree.

- "Revenue/cost performance centers" will be developed to provide accountability by college, school, residence, research, curriculum, discipline, and special programs. The resulting data will be invaluable for financial control, strategic planning, and mission realignment.

- Tuition prices will stabilize, or decrease, to a fair asking price in today's market. Tuition discounts will be reduced to reflect successful cost containment programs. Lower discounts will allow higher education to resume traditional scholarship programs.

Higher education is a major industry in the United States, and certainly at the top of the list as regards long-term continued development of the nation. In order to maintian its world stature, and affordibility for our citizens, American higher education must assume a competitive posture in the same manner that industry in this country did during the past 15 years.

FOR FURTHER READING

Anderson, Richard E., and Meyerson, Joel W., eds. *Productivity and Higher Education: Improving the Effectiveness of Faculty, Facilities and Financial Resources*. Princeton, NJ: Peterson's Guides, Inc., 1992.

Firstenberg, Paul B. *Managing For-Profit in the Non-Profit World*. New York: The Foundation Center, 1986.

Seymour, Daniel T. *On Q: Causing Quality in Higher Education*. American Council on Education/Oryx Press Series on Higher Education. Phoenix, AZ: Oryx Press, 1992.

BIBLIOGRAPHY

• • • • • • • • •

ARTICLES

Chabotar, Kent John, and Honan, James P. "Coping with Retrenchment: Strategies and Tactics." *Change* (November/December 1990): 28-34.

Contracting for Facilities Service. No. 9 in the Critical Issues Facilities Management Series, foreword by Sean C. Rush. Alexandria, VA: *Association for Physical Plant Administrators,* 1995.

Deutschman, Alan. "Why Universities Are Shrinking." *Fortune* (24 September 1990): 103–08.

Dunn, John A., Jr. "How Colleges Should Handle Their Endowment." *Planning for Higher Education* 19 (Spring 1991): 32-37.

"Federal Contracts Report." *Bureau of National Affairs.* (15 July 1991).

Hacker, Andrew. "Too Many Full Professors: A Top-Heavy Pyramid." *The Chronicle of Higher Education* (4 March 1992): B1-B2.

Hawkins, Brian L. "Preparing for the Next Wave of Computers on Campus." *Change* (January/February 1991): 24-31.

Hubbel, Loren Loomis. "Tuition Discounting: The Impact of Institutionally Funded Financial Aid." Washington, DC: National Association of College and University Business Officers, 1992.

Hubbel, Loren Loomis, and Sean C. Rush. "A Double-Edged Sword: Assessing the Impact of Tuition Discounting." Washington, DC: National Association of College and University Business Officers, 1991.

Johnson, Sandra L., and Meyerson, Joel W. "More Top Concerns for 1992." *AGB Reports* (January/February 1992): 11-15.

Kerr, Thomas J. "College Tuition: Collusion or Compromise?" *School & College* (June 1990): 11–16.

Kramer, Martin. "Money and Race Relations: Toward a Color Blind Financial Aid System." *Change* (May/June 1991): 53-54.

Langfitt, Thomas W. "The Costs of Higher Education: Lessons to Learn from the Health Care Industry." *Change* (November/December 1990): 8-15.

Leslie, Connie. "The Public Ivy Is Withering." *Newsweek* (29 April 1991): 64-65.

Likins, Peter. "Doing More with Less." *Eastern Association of College and University Business Officers Newsletter* (Winter 1992): 6-8.

Massy, William F., and Zemsky, Robert. "Cost Containment: Committing to a New Economic Reality." *Change* (November/December 1990): 16-22.

McPherson, Michael S., and Schapiro, Morton Owen. "The Student Finance System for Undergraduate Education: How Well Does It Work?" *Change* (May/June 1991): 16-22.

Mooney, Carol J. "As Wave of Curricular Reform Continues, Its Scope and Effectiveness Are Questioned." *The Chronicle of Higher Education* (8 January 1992): A15-A18.

Sheler, Jeffery L., et al. "A New Era on Campus." *U.S. News and World Report* (16 October 1989): 54-57.

Shuart, James M. "One View of the Near Future in Higher Education." KPMG Peat Marwick *Management Issues for Colleges and Universities* (July 1989): 1-3.

"Trends and Indicators." *The Chronicle of Higher Education.* (25 March 1992): A16.

BOOKS

Anderson, Charles J., Carter, Deborah J., and Malizio, Andrew G. *1989-1990 Fact Book on Higher Education.* American Council on Education/Oryx Press Series on Higher Education. Phoenix, AZ: Oryx Press, 1989.

Anderson, Richard E., and Joel W. Meyerson, eds. *Financing Higher Education in a Global Economy.* American Council on Education/Oryx Press Series on Higher Education. Phoenix, AZ: Oryx Press, 1990.

———. *Productivity and Higher Education: Improving the Effectiveness of Faculty, Facilities, and Financial Resources.* Princeton, NJ: Peterson's Guides, Inc., 1992.

Anthony, Robert N., and Herzlinger, Regina E., eds. *Management Control in Nonprofit Organizations.* Homewood, IL: Richard D. Irwin, Inc., 1975.

Bensimon, Estela M.; Neumann, Anna; and Birnbaum, Robert. *Making Sense of Administrative Leadership: The 'L' Word in Higher Education.* ASHE-ERIC Higher Education Report no. 1. Washington, DC: School of Education and Human Development, The George Washington University, 1989.

Bowen, Howard R. *The Costs of Higher Education: How Much Do Colleges and Universities Spend Per Student and How Much Should They Spend?* San Francisco: Jossey-Bass, Publishers, 1980.

Buhler-Miko, Marina. *A Trustee's Guide to Strategic Planning*. Washington, DC: Higher Education Strategic Planning Institute, 1985.

Bulloch, James; Keller, Donald E.; and Vlasho, Louis, eds. *Accountants' Cost Handbook: A Guide for Management Accounting*. 3d ed. New York: John Wiley and Sons, 1983.

Castaldi, Basil. *Educational Facilities: Planning, Remodeling, and Management*. Boston: Allyn and Bacon, Inc., 1977.

College and University Business Administration. 3d ed. Washington, DC: National Association of College and University Business Officers, 1974.

Cope, Robert G. *Opportunity from Strength: Strategic Planning Clarified with Case Examples*. ASHE-ERIC Higher Education Report no. 8. Washington, DC: Association for the Study of Higher Education, 1987.

Feasley, Charles E. *Serving Learners at a Distance: A Guide to Program Practices*. ASHE-ERIC Higher Education Research Report no. 5. Washington, DC: Association for the Study of Higher Education, 1983.

Firstenberg, Paul B. *Managing for Profit in the Nonprofit World*. New York: The Foundation Center, 1986.

Fisher, James L. *The Board and the President*. American Council on Education/Oryx Press Series on Higher Education. Phoenix, AZ: Oryx Press, 1991.

Fisher, James L., and Quehl, Gary H. *The President and Fund Raising*. American Council on Education/Oryx Press Series on Higher Education. Phoenix, AZ: Oryx Press, 1989.

Fisher, James L.; Tack, Martha W.; and Wheeler, Karen J. *Effective College President*. American Council on Education/Oryx Press Series on Higher Education. Phoenix, AZ: 1988.

Froomkin, Joseph, ed. *The Crisis in Higher Education*. Montpelier Capital, VT: City Press, 1983.

Gambino, Anthony J. *Planning and Control in Higher Education*. New York: National Association of Accountants, 1979.

Ginsburg, Sigmund G., and Karol, Nathaniel H. *Managing the Higher Education Enterprise*. New York: John Wiley & Sons, 1980.

Harasim, Linda M., ed. *Online Education Perspectives on a New Environment*. New York: Praeger Publishers, 1990.

Hauptman, Arthur M. *The Tuition Dilemma*. Washington, DC: The Brookings Institution, 1990.

Ingram, Richard T., and Associates. *Handbook of College and University Trusteeship*. San Francisco: Jossey-Bass Publishers, 1980.

Kaiser, Harvey. *The Facilities Audit*. Alexandria, VA: Association for Physical Plant Administrators, 1994.

Keller, George. *Academic Strategy: The Management Revolution in American Higher Education*. Baltimore: The John Hopkins University Press, 1983.

Kotler, Philip and Karen F. Fox. *Strategic Marketing for Educational Institutions.* Englewood Cliffs, NJ: Prentice-Hall, Inc., 1985.

Kurzig, Carol M. *Foundation Fundamentals: A Guide for Grant Seekers.* New York: The Foundation Center, 1980.

Layzell, Daniel T., and Lyddon, Jan W. *Budgeting for Higher Education at the State Level: Enigma, Paradox, and Ritual.* ASHE-ERIC Higher Education Report no. 4. Washington, DC: The George Washington University, 1990.

Lefferts, Robert. *The Basic Handbook of Grants Management.* New York: Basic Books, Inc., 1983.

Litten, Larry H.; Sullivan, Daniel; and Brodigan, David L. *Applying Market Research in College Admissions.* New York: College Entrance Examination Board, 1983.

Locke, Lawrence F.; Spirduso, Woneen Wyrick; and Silverman, Stephen J. *Proposals That Work: A Guide for Planning Dissertations and Grant Proposals.* Newbury Park, CA: Sage Publications, 1987.

Managing the Facilities Portfolio. Washington, DC: National Association of College and University Business Officers, 1991.

Massy, William F. *Endowment: Perspectives, Policies, and Management.* Washington, DC: Association of Governing Boards of Universities and Colleges, 1990.

Mortimer, Kenneth P.; Bagshaw, Marque; and Masland, Andrew T. *Flexibility in Academic Staffing: Effective Policies and Practices.* ASHE-ERIC Higher Education Report no. 1. Washington, DC: Association for the Study of Higher Education, 1985.

National Center for Educational Statistics. *Projections of Higher Education Statistics to 2002.* Washington, DC: U.S. Department of Educational Research and Improvement, NCES 91-490, 1991.

National Symposium on Strategic Higher Education Finance and Management Issues: Proceedings. Washington, DC: National Association of College and University Business Officers, 1991.

Nevin, Jeanne, ed. *Management of Student Aid.* Washington, DC: National Association of College and University Business Officers, 1979.

Ostar, Roberta H. *Public Roles, Private Lives: The Representational Role of College and University Presidents.* AGB Special Reports, 1991.

Paulsen, Michael B. *College Choice: Understanding Student Enrollment Behavior.* ASHE-ERIC Higher Education Report no. 6. Washington, DC: The George Washington University, School of Education and Human Development, 1990.

Perun, Pamela J. *The Undergraduate Woman: Issues in Educational Equity.* Lexington, MA: D.C. Heath and Co., 1982.

Plante, Patricia R., with Caret, Robert L. *Myths and Realities of Academic Administration*. American Council on Education/Oryx Press Series on Higher Education. Phoenix, AZ: Oryx Press, 1990.

Presidential Search: A Guide to the Process of Selecting and Appointing College and University Presidents. Washington, DC: Association of Governing Boards of Universities and Colleges, 1979.

Robinson, Daniel D. *Capital Maintenance for Colleges and Universities*. Washington, DC: National Association of College and University Business Officers, 1986.

Seymour, Daniel T. *On Q: Causing Quality in Higher Education*. American Council on Education/Oryx Press Series on Higher Education. Phoenix, AZ: Oryx Press, 1993.

Silva, Paul V. *Unitizing Investment Pools*. Accounting Guidebook Series. Washington, DC: National Association of College and University Business Offices, 1993.

Sykes, Charles J. *Prof Scam: Professors and the Demise of Higher Education*. New York: St. Martin's Press, 1988.

Taylor, Barbara E. *Working Effectively with Trustees: Building Cooperative Campus Leadership*. ASHE-ERIC Higher Education Report no. 2. Washington, DC: Association for the Study of Higher Education, 1987.

Turk, Frederick J. "Activity Based Costing." *National Symposium on Strategic Higher Education Finance & Management Issues: Proceedings*. Washington, DC: National Association of College and University Business Officers, 1991.

U.S. Department of Education. *Tough Choices: A Guide to Administrative Cost Management in Colleges and Universities*. Washington, DC: Department of Education, 1991.

Walker, Donald E. *The Effective Administrator: A Practical Approach to Problem Solving, Decision Making, and Campus Leadership*. San Francisco: Jossey-Bass Publishers, 1979.

INDEX

· · · · · · · · ·

by Kay Banning